I0009111

WE CHOOSE TO GO TO THE MOON

A FIRST-PERSON NARRATIVE OF THE DEVELOPMENT PROCESS BEHIND
BUZZ ALDRIN'S SPACE PROGRAM MANAGER

To my parents and my sister

ACKNOWLEDGMENTS

The writing of this book wasn't by any means an individual effort. In no particular order, I'd like to thank the following individuals for their contributions to this book.

I'd like to thank John Curtis, Gregory Mack and Steve Lohr, members of Space Program Manager community, for providing feedback on the early drafts of this manuscript.

I'd also like to thank Brittany Gall and Nancy Callegary, for performing a thorough editing of the text.

Thanks to Mauricio Sanjurjo, the 3D artist of Space Program Manager and my current development partner, for creating the cover art and the layout of this book.

A big thanks to my grandfather Ernesto Ejarque, who was always very supportive of my side projects. Sadly, he left us in early May 2015, though I'm grateful because he lived long enough to see the release of Space Program Manager.

Last but not least, I would like to thank my family, for always being and endless stream of support.

TABLE OF CONTENTS

Part I
[2007 until 2010]

Part II
[2011 until 2013]

Part III
[2014 until 2015]

Part IV
[Lessons Learned While Developing SPM]

Epilogue

PART I [2007 UNTIL 2010]

Introduction

After nearly eight years of development, Buzz Aldrin's Space Program Manager (hereafter referred to as "SPM") finally saw the light of day at the end of October 2014 on Windows and Mac, and in March 2015 on iPad devices. It was a very long process, which started as a personal hobby when I was 22 years old. I'll be celebrating my 32nd birthday next March so, in a sense, one can say that SPM is a project that has been with me during my whole adult life!

SPM is a strategy game for both desktop and mobile platforms where the player assumes the role of Director of either NASA or the Soviet Space Agency and has to carefully manage the budget and all their various resources in order to be the first to achieve a manned lunar landing mission. The game was developed under the "Polar Motion" brand and published by Slitherine Ltd, a publishing house of strategy games located in Epsom, just outside West London. The game went through a one-year Early Access Program that started in October 2013, where the game was available for purchase on Slitherine's online store. The release version is now available for purchase both in the publisher's <u>online store</u>[1] and on <u>Steam</u>[2].

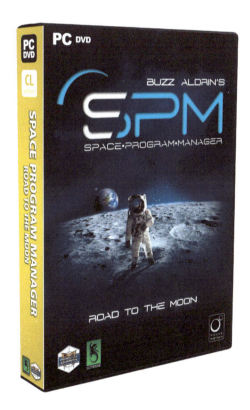

- "Buzz Aldrin's Space Program Manager" box art. -

I started writing the first draft for a post-mortem around Christmas 2014, nearly two months after the desktop release. Then I realised that it was too soon for me to start writing such a document, so I decided to wait for a few more months and let the remaining critical events, such as the release for mobile platforms, unfold. I believe this was the right call because, had I gone ahead and published a post-mortem at that time, I'd have had to write an addendum not long afterwards!

Now that the dust has settled and while the memories are still fresh in my mind, I believe it's a good idea to write down a narrative covering all the major events that took place during the development process of SPM. Not only to share my experiences with other fellow developers but also to put a personal closure on what has been an extremely lengthy project.

This narrative will depart from the traditional "what went right/what went wrong" structure found in most post-mortem articles. Instead, I'll describe all the major events related to the project that took place since I started working on it in early 2007. I'll also provide some background information about both my personal situation and the way I perceived the industry landscape so that you can get a better understanding of the rationale behind some of the decisions I made. Some of them turned out to be right, others not so much, and a few were just downright silly. I find that writing all these things down is one of the best ways to organise the ideas in my head, learn and, more importantly, make sure I won't make the same mistakes in the future. I hope that this book will be a resource for my readers, to give you guidance, advice, and some insight into the game industry.

Even though the circumstances of each project are unique, I really hope some of the lessons I'm sharing here will be useful to other fellow game developers too. Since I was directly involved in all areas during the development process behind SPM, either by doing things myself or by working closely with the other members of my team, I believe this book can offer a comprehensive view of the development process behind a medium-complexity game made by a very small development team.

A quick summary about myself: my name is Ignacio Liverotti and I was the Lead Developer behind SPM. I was born in Argentina and earned a degree in Computer Science Engineering from the Buenos Aires Institute of Technology (ITBA) in 2009. I've held a variety of software development jobs across various domains, such as console games and air traffic control simulators. I emigrated to the UK in mid-2011 and I'm currently living in the Brighton and Hove area, where I work as a Software Developer for Unity Technologies Ltd. as part of its Sustained Engineering team.

The Inception (January and February 2007)

The development of SPM started as a hobby project in January 2007, a couple of weeks after I began my first internship as a software developer at a small company in Buenos Aires. I was a full-time student working towards a 5-year degree in Computer Science Engineering but, at the end of 2006, I decided that I was going to enroll in fewer courses during the following academic year and apply to a part-time job so that I could gain some relevant work experience. The job involved developing software in C++ for industrial PDAs powered by the Pocket PC/Windows Mobile operating systems. My first assignment was to develop an SSH 2 client for those devices based on the documentation available across various RFCs. It was a great job and I really enjoyed it.

Regarding my background in games, I used to play the Famicom when I was a kid, which was a very popular console in my native Argentina during the early 1990s. During my early teens, I also had an N64. Around mid-2000, while still in High School, I became quite curious about how games were made, and my interests shifted from playing them to actually learning the skills required to make them. By the end of that year, I managed to persuade my parents to buy me a PC, and so I started teaching myself the C programming language.

- The 3D software rasterizer displaying an MD2 model of Yoshi. -

By mid-2001, I devoted many hours to my interest in game programming and teaching myself C++, the Windows API, and DirectX. In the subsequent years, I'd also work on a variety of "pet projects" such as a 2D platform game for the Game Boy Advance handheld and a texture mapped 3D software rasterizer capable of displaying Quake 2 MD2 files. I wasn't much into playing games, but I found the challenge of learning the techniques required to make them and applying that knowledge to side projects very exciting.

I hoped that someday I would be able to join the game industry after graduating from College and be able to work on big-budget game titles. I used to see all the fast-paced progress in graphics technologies for games that was taking place and I couldn't help but think about how realistic and awesome they were going to look by the time I graduated. I saw a lot of potential opportunities there and I definitely wanted to be part of the industry after obtaining my degree.

In late 2003, right before starting my freshman year in College, I began developing an interest in the space race. I was mainly focused on the Apollo program, the Lunar Landings and because of that, I re-discovered "Buzz Aldrin's Race into Space" (a.k.a. "BARIS"). BARIS is a 1993 DOS game I had heard about when I was a kid, but that I never had the chance to play. By that time, Interplay, the game's publisher, had already given back the rights to its creator, Fritz Bronner, who kindly made the game freely available on the web.

- "Buzz Aldrin's Race Into Space" title screen.-

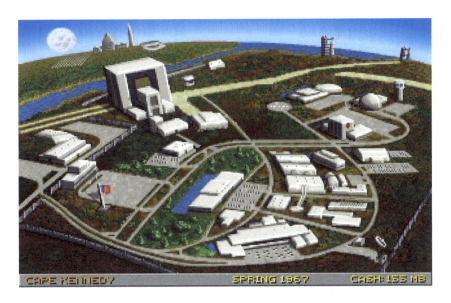

CAPE KENNEDY   SPRING 1967   CASH: 155 MB

- "Buzz Aldrin's Race Into Space" American space complex screen.-

BARIS is a strategy game where the player would lead the efforts of either NASA or the Soviet Union in order to be the first to land a man on the Moon and bring him safely back to Earth. BARIS was the computer version of a board game called LIFTOFF! (also by Bronner) and it featured some impressive technical achievements, such as animated video clips that portrayed the sequence of events for the various space missions. This was back in a time where the word "multimedia" was all the rage.

The player is shown a fixed view of the space complex and visits the various buildings spread across the landscape in order to perform a series of tasks such as opening programs, assigning R&D teams to improve the hardware's reliability, hire astronauts, schedule missions and much more. In real life, NASA is not based on a single location but is instead spread across several states. Likewise, the Soviet space efforts didn't fall under a single, all-encompassing entity. There were actually several Bureaus who competed with each other for resources. Modelling this complexity inside the game would have resulted in a very poor gameplay experience, so the designer placed all the various elements of each space program under a single space complex.

We took the exact same approach on SPM. Though I must say that the implementation of the space complex in the original BARIS is superior to ours, as it features animations and various other small details that makes the whole execution feel a lot tighter.

- "Buzz Aldrin's Race Into Space" research and development screen.-

The mission video clips are based on edited NASA footage and, even though the game would sometimes play audio from a manned mission when depicting the events of an unmanned one, it provided a very immersive experience which is still fondly remembered more than 20 years later by its fans. Creating all these animated sequences must have been a very laborious process for the original developers in the early 1990s. Coincidentally, creating the animations featured in SPM was an extremely laborious process for us as well in 2013.

I won't write a full analysis of the original BARIS though I would like to say that it is a very well executed game, and remains an engaging product that has aged remarkably well. The game gets some major things right and creates a great and immersive atmosphere that really captures the essence of the "Race to the Moon".

- The Saturn V launch sequence in "Buzz Aldrin's Race Into Space".-

Even though I found BARIS very fun to play, what I found really appealing was the fact that it encouraged me to go out and learn more about space exploration and the space race from other sources, such as books and documentaries. I was very intrigued by the fact that it had never been remade and/or extended in scope by, for example, adding space stations in Earth orbit or a manned Mission to Mars. I started sketching some ideas for a remake in early 2004, but then my first year at College began and I found myself devoting nearly all my waking hours to it. Thus, I had to momentarily put my plans for a BARIS remake on hold.

When I had finally managed to get the hang of College and was going through my first software development job, I decided it was time for me to embark on another pet project to hone my skills and improve my chances of getting a job in games after graduation. On a very broad level, the project had the following two goals and requirements:

1. It had to be reasonably sized in scope. Not so small that it would end up being labelled as "irrelevant", but not so big that I would never be able to finish it. In my book, reasonably-sized finished projects always win against ambitious ones that are eventually abandoned due to lack of motivation or interest.

2. It had to be an excellent addition to my portfolio. Something that, at the very least, would allow me to land a job interview at a games studio.

With these goals in mind, I decided to resurrect my plans for a BARIS remake. The four initial requirements for this remake were as follows:

1. It would extend the scope of the original game by going beyond the Lunar Landings and featuring elements of the current space program, such as modular space stations, along with futuristic elements like a manned mission to Mars. Unlike the original game, though, the remake wouldn't feature the "Race to the Moon". Thus, the competition aspect would be scrapped and replaced with a focus on exploration.

2. It would feature lots of heavily researched text.

3. All graphics would be custom-made; we would use the historical footage as a reference only.

4. The game mechanics would be relatively straightforward, featuring a simple set of systems where the player can easily understand what's happening behind the scenes.

Each of these initial requirements had a specific rationale behind them.

1. **Extending the scope of the original game and discarding the "Race to the Moon":** The original BARIS did an excellent job of capturing the essence of the "Race to the Moon" and, while the idea of extending it beyond the Lunar Landings is a good one, I realised that creating original content for each faction would have required tremendous production values. I concluded that it would be better to deliver something that the original BARIS didn't, yet keep the production costs at a reasonable level.

2. **Lots of heavily researched content:** I wanted the game to show and describe in detail the various elements of the space program, such as the hardware (rockets, space probes, manned spacecraft, etc.) and the missions. The game, just like the original BARIS, was meant to be fun to play, but I also wanted players to learn the details about the various space missions along the way and, hopefully, inspire them to learn even more from other sources.

3. **Custom-made content:** BARIS managed to deliver an immersive experience by using the historical footage for the base of the game. Since SPM was working beyond the Lunar Landings, we would have to create our own content for those missions where there isn't any historical footage available.

4. **Simple and straightforward mechanics:** As the only programmer for this project, I made a conscious decision to keep the game mechanics as simple and straightforward as possible. Not only because simpler mechanics made the code easier to write, debug and maintain, but also because I knew balancing a game with tons of moving parts can be extremely time-consuming, and I wouldn't have the time to do that.

Preliminary Work (March - October 2007)

The new semester in college started in March, and I enrolled in two eight-credit courses which, along with my day job as a software developer intern, left me with only a handful of hours per week to work on my side project, so I tried to make the most out of them.

The project already had a name: "Space Program Manager", and it would feature a 3D map similar to the one from BARIS, the only difference is that the map in SPM would be rendered in real-time. The player would be in charge of a fictional space agency named GSA, an acronym for "Global Space Agency", which would feature programs from NASA, the Soviet Space Agency and some probes from other space agencies such as ESA and JAXA. Just like in BARIS, the player would visit the various buildings from the space agency to perform administrative tasks such as opening programs, investing R&D funds in order to develop hardware, schedule missions, recruit astronauts, etc. The video sequences from BARIS would be replaced by scripted animations featuring low-poly 3D models which, just like the original game, would depict the most important phases from each mission. Players would also be able to rotate the camera around and zoom in/out when watching the animations, which I believed would be a very nice feature.

Regarding the underlying technology, unfortunately in 2007 there weren't that many low-cost tools and game engines available. As far as open-source engines went, there was OGRE, which had a considerably steep learning curve, and there was Irrlicht, which was a bit more accessible and straightforward. Commercial engines were not an option; the low-cost ones, such as Torque, were not suitable for the type of game I wanted to make. The high-profile ones, such as Unreal and idTech, were so expensive that they were definitely out of the question, and probably not entirely suitable for SPM either. Nowadays there's a plethora of options available and Unreal, which would have cost a fortune upfront just eight years ago, is now freely available, along with its source code and all its tools. Again, another example of the radical changes in the landscape that have occurred in the last decade!

In the end, I went for Irrlicht: its API was in C++, a language I was already familiar with, the documentation was good, it performed well across a broad range of hardware combinations and it featured lots of examples to learn from.

With a rough idea of the type of game I wanted to make and my game engine decision, I spent this period creating a spreadsheet of all the elements that would

- Irrlicht's main feature list, circa March 2007.-

be available throughout the game. I then began sketching the details of the UI on paper, laid out the source code structure and did some small technical tests on the side to de-risk some areas.

At the end of this period, I also began looking for freelance artists to do a small set of low-poly 3D models for the various spacecraft. I posted a message on a local online forum and, within a few days, I got a considerable amount of replies from various artists interested in getting more details about the project. After getting their quotes and exchanging e-mails in order to nail down the details, I selected one who was also living in Buenos Aires. We met in person, agreed on the details of the work package, including the cost for each model, and the work commenced.

As days went by, we exchanged e-mails to discuss and resolve all the issues that were cropping up, ones that could be expected in this kind of work. And then, a mere few weeks later, I got an e-mail from him stating that the models were taking longer to produce than he had originally anticipated and that he felt he should have priced the work package higher.

I decided to cancel the work altogether and take a step back to look at the drawing board again. Fortunately, I only lost a small amount of money and, in a sense, this first experience of hiring someone was very positive, since it gave me a glimpse of what to expect when liaising with contractors.

Let's Go Portable (November - December 2007)

Influenced by my exposure to mobile devices on a daily basis at my internship, and the fact that the PC market in 2007 didn't seem very appealing, I decided to reduce the scope of the game and target mobile devices. More specifically, the Pocket PC and Windows Mobile platforms. This was right after the first iPhone was released, but before the App Store was available for regular developers. As crazy as it sounds when looking at it through a 2015 lens, it was a time when there was a market with customers willing to pay somewhere between $5 and $7 to play a simple, yet polished, puzzle game on their PDAs.

The clickgamer.com frontpage, circa October 2008 (retrieved using the Wayback Machine)

The game would still be called "Space Program Manager" and the player would still have to manage a fictional space agency featuring elements from all the major space agencies, but it would be played on a small screen. The original plan of producing scripted animations featuring low-poly 3D models was scrapped and I decided to replace it with a slideshow of static 2D images, with a pinch of sprite-based animations for some sections in a few places in order to spice things up. This approach, I reasoned, would be a lot less expensive to produce than the scripted low-poly 3D models.

At the end of 2007, I started to investigate the various tools available and decided to adopt a multi-platform game engine named "Edgelib" which, under the slogan of "Mobilize your code!", provided a unified C++ interface that could target PC, Linux, Pocket PC, Windows Mobile Smartphone, Symbian, GP2X and various other platforms. It wasn't as nearly as simple to use as Unity and other various game engines and libraries available nowadays, but it allowed me to do the development on my PC using Microsoft Visual C++ and then recompile it under Embedded Visual C++ to target Pocket PC and Windows Mobile, and that's all I needed.

- The Edgelib webpage at the end of 2007 (retrieved using the Wayback Machine).-

At that time, Edgelib was commercialised under a yearly subscription model, which allowed the user "to create and release as many commercial games and applications as desired for all supported platforms during the licensing period". That being said, the subscription was very expensive for me (especially taking into account that the Argentinian Peso is very weak against the Euro), so I went ahead and downloaded their evaluation version, which featured nearly all the functionality of the paid version minus the ability to release a commercial product with it. I didn't know how long it would take me to develop and release the game (or even if I was going to be able to release it at all!), so I decided to worry about completing its development first and worrying about middleware licensing later.

- The Edgelib licensing webpage at the end of 2007 (retrieved using the Wayback Machine).-

At the end of 2007, my internship ended and, even though I really liked my job and I could have stayed at the company in a permanent position, I decided to go back to college as a full-time student in order to complete the remaining courses required for my computer science engineering degree.

Getting Serious (January - August 2008)

In the summer vacation of 2008, which takes place during January and February in the Southern Hemisphere, I started porting my code to the Edgelib library. Since the library didn't feature a UI system, I had to roll my own, which I tested using placeholder assets.

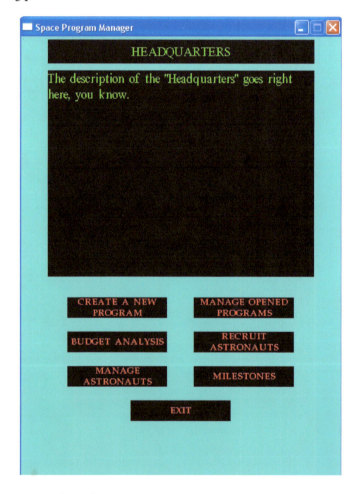

- The Headquarters screen using placeholder artwork and text.-

WE CHOOSE TO GO TO THE MOON

The system was very primitive when compared to the various tools available nowadays. Nonetheless, it provided a degree of flexibility by allowing me to define the various UI elements such as static images, text overlays and buttons in an XML file and quickly perform any minor tweaks without having to recompile the source code.

```xml
SPMGmStMainCentersHQ.xml
1    <GUIElements GUIThemeID='0' FontFileID='0'>
2
3    <GUIElement> <!-- Background image -->
4     <Ctg>StaticImage</Ctg>
5     <C>0</C>
6     <C>0</C>
7     <C>1023</C>
8     <C>767</C>
9     <Parent>0</Parent>
10    <ImgID>207</ImgID>
11    <ID>600</ID>
12   </GUIElement>
13
14   <GUIElement> <!-- HEADQUARTERS -->
15    <Ctg>TextOverlay</Ctg>
16    <ID>601</ID>
17    <TypeID>0</TypeID>
18    <Parent>0</Parent>
19    <Corners C1='512' C2='50' C3='514' C4='50'/>
20    <TextString ID='0'/>
21   </GUIElement>
22
23   <GUIElement> <!-- Headquarters image -->
24    <Ctg>StaticImage</Ctg>
25    <C>40</C>
26    <C>115</C>
27    <C>985</C>
28    <C>235</C>
29    <Parent>0</Parent>
30    <ImgID>-1</ImgID>
31    <ID>602</ID>
32   </GUIElement>
33
34   <GUIElement> <!-- Description -->
35    <Ctg>StaticTextScrollable</Ctg>
36    <ID>603</ID>
37    <TypeID>1</TypeID>
38    <Parent>0</Parent>
39    <Corners C1='55' C2='275' C3='494' C4='575'/>
40    <TextCorners C1='10' C2='8' C3='430' C4='-1'/>
41    <TextString ID='8'/>
42   </GUIElement>
43
44   <GUIElement> <!-- CREATE A NEW PROGRAM -->
45    <Ctg>Button</Ctg>
46    <ID>604</ID>
47    <TypeID>30</TypeID>
```

- A snippet of the XML file that defines the layout of the Headquarters screen.-

That being said, the system had its shortcomings, and I made some sub-optimal design decisions during its development. If I had another go at it, here are the two major things that I'd do differently:

1. I'd write an editor in C# using WinForms or WPF so that I could edit the layout visually instead of by punching numbers into a text file. By having such a tool, not only would I be able to iterate the screen layouts at a faster rate but also, I'd be able to let an artist do the final tweaking of the various UI elements without having to be personally involved in the project.

2. I'd design the system so that the various UI widgets are defined in terms of anchors and screen percentages, instead of defining them by using pixels. This way, the UI will adapt itself well to multiple resolutions and aspect ratios.

By the end of February, I contacted a freelance web developer I found online to help me replace my placeholder assets with proper artwork. We exchanged a few e-mails and he really liked the concept behind the game. His only condition was that he would only work remotely, something I was perfectly happy with since I didn't have any office space anyway!

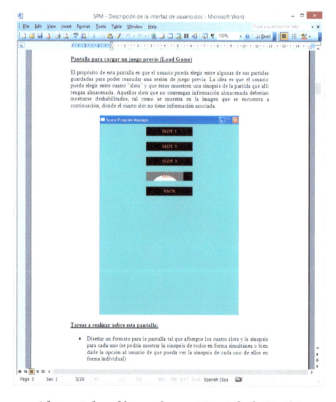

- A fragment of one of the specs documents I wrote for the UI artist.-

This phase went pretty smoothly; I'd write documents describing what needed to be done, and we'd clarify any issues via e-mail and chat. He charged me a sensible amount of money for his work and took into account that, in the end, I was a student who was financing this project out of his own pocket. I was very pleased with the screens he produced and, to this day, I still think they looked quite stylish for a 2008 game.

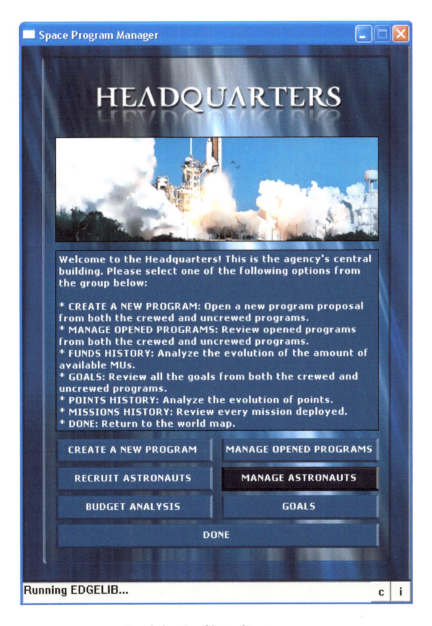

- Reworked version of the Headquarters screen.-

At some point, while we were working on the UI, I told him my plans to depict the in-game missions using a set of static 2D images that would be created from scratch. He said that showing static images was a good idea, but suggested an alternative approach; instead of creating each image from scratch, why not invest a bit more time upfront, create a set of 3D models for all spacecraft and arrange said models in different ways to create the various static images? This was an ingenious approach. To be honest, I was a bit embarrassed about the fact that I wasn't the one that came up with it!

The new semester at College started in March and I enrolled in a set of demanding courses such as Computer Graphics, Artificial Intelligence and Compiler Construction and Design. Unlike the previous year, though, I had a more flexible schedule, so I was able to alternate my daily schedule between SPM and my coursework.

I posted once again a message in a local online forum, this time looking for an artist who could make the 3D models for the various spacecraft required for the game. Unlike the previous year, the models wouldn't have to be optimised for real-time rendering, so that made the pool of potential candidates bigger. After exchanging some e-mails, the final arrangement involved a 3D artist who would create the geometry for each model and a separate group of artists who would take said models and create and apply the textures to them. Surprisingly, this arrangement worked very well, despite the fact that both parties never met in person or even exchanged a single e-mail, as I always acted as the proxy between them.

-The 3D model for the Pioneer 6, 7, 8 and 9 probes.-

The remaining months during this period were very productive; the 3D artists managed to get over forty 3D models done at a rate of around five models per week and I made quite a lot of progress in the development of the C++ prototype. I also hired a 2D artist to create the assets for the various buildings in the space complex.

-The 3D model for the Skylab space station, along with a docked Apollo CSM.-

-Draft showing the tentative location of the various buildings of the space complex in 640x840 portrait resolution.-

-The sprite for the Vehicle Assembly Building.-

Intermezzo: Flip Disc (September 2008 - Early May 2009)

During 2008, I realised that it would probably take a while before SPM would be completed, so I decided to put the project aside for a while and create a simpler game in order to gain experience by going through the whole development process, from inception to release.

My game of choice was "Flip Disc", which was based on a prototype I had made at the end of 2003 using C++ and DirectX 6. "Flip Disc" is an original design, which can be described as a "circular Tetris". In a nutshell, the game features a circular board with eight lanes. Coloured balls are constantly showing up from the outer area of the board and the player has to align those that share the same colour by rotating a group of concentric discs. The "Flip" part of the name is there because the player is also able to "mirror" the currently selected disc across the axis determined by the two small lines located outside the board, which can also be rotated. This gameplay mechanic didn't make it into the final game. Nonetheless, I decided to keep the name "Flip Disc" because it sounded catchy.

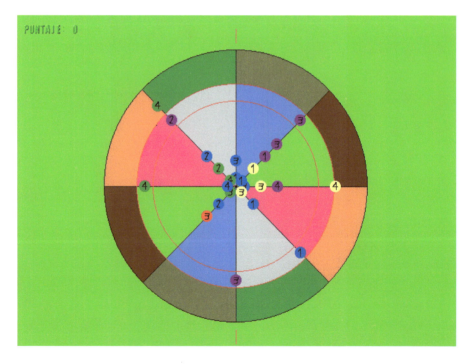

-Flip Disc original prototype (December 2003).-

Such a simple game would be a hard sell in the highly-competitive mobile space of 2015, and C++ is certainly not best tool if the end goal is to ship a product quickly. However, the landscape in mid-2008 was completely different to today's, as mobile games were not nearly as ambitious, and the range of available development tools was not nearly as wide. In any case, the main objective behind the development of Flip Disc was to gain experience developing a full product and releasing it.

I posted a new message on a local online forum to look for a freelance artist willing to take my existing prototype and "spice up" the graphics. One artist contacted me right away and sent me a proof of concept which looked very promising. As a bonus, he also had experience developing games for mobile platforms and had a good grasp of the requirements and limitations that handheld devices place on the artwork. After exchanging a couple of e-mails, I decided to hire him. I also hired a musician to produce catchy tunes and sound effects for the game.

The development of Flip Disc went quite smoothly, and I was able to work on it during the evenings and in whichever time slots I managed to find between college assignments, midterms, and final exams. The game was finally released on December 25th, 2008 on the clickgamer.com website for Windows desktop and PocketPC/Windows Mobile. It featured support for QVGA (320x240) and VGA (640x480) resolutions on mobile devices, and a fixed 1024x768 resolution for the PC version. The game spanned ten levels, each with its own unique background tune, and a few new gameplay elements that were not present in the original prototype, such as "special" gems.

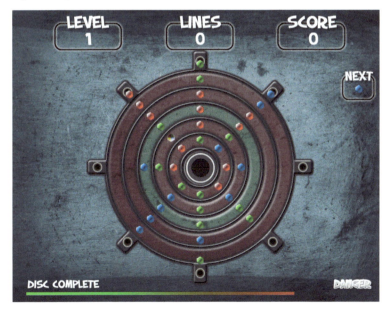

-Flip Disc main gameplay screen - PC version (December 2008).-

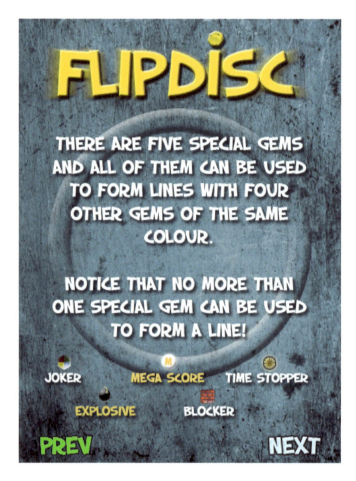

-Flip Disc original prototype (December 2003).-

At the beginning of 2009, I exchanged a couple of e-mails with the owners of clickgamer.com, who encouraged me to port my game to iPhone claiming that "it's the future". They really knew what they were talking about, as during the next couple of years they would publish several hit titles on the platform and until they were eventually acquired by Electronic Arts.

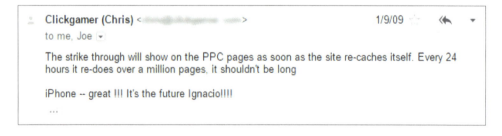

-Encouragement e-mail from one of Chillingo's owners regarding an iPhone port of Flip Disc (January 2009).-

-Flip Disc 1.0 for iPhone OS, featuring soft buttons for input (March 2009).-

-Flip Disc 1.0.1 for iPhone OS (circa May 2009).-

With a used MacBook and an iPod Touch I managed to get hold of, I ported the game to iOS (then called "iPhone OS"), which was a fascinating challenge from a technical point of view, as I had to learn how to use a Mac along with the basics of Objective-C. The game was finally released in the App Store in March 2009 and was subsequently updated a couple of months later with a new version featuring enhanced graphics and input controls.

Despite getting some coverage on various websites and even a video review on YouTube [3], Flip Disc failed to gain traction and only sold a handful of copies. To be honest, this wasn't a surprise and, even with all the "happy go lucky" stories that were reported in the media during the early days of the iPhone platform, I never expected Flip Disc to be a ground-breaking commercial success. That being said, it was a significant accomplishment, as I proved to myself that I could develop a complete game from scratch.

Being such a simple game, it doesn't deserve to have its own post-mortem. Nonetheless, here's a short summary of the key takeaways from this experience:

- Always keep a single codebase for all platforms. Use conditional compilation to hide any platform-specific details, but try to keep as much code in the common area as possible. This way, there would be less code to maintain, and any bug fix or optimisation introduced will automatically make its way to all the target platforms.

- Write custom tools to automate common tasks, such as assets conversion and installer creation. This reduces the time it takes to deploy new versions while also reducing the amount of errors by ensuring that no steps from the build process are omitted.

- Do the bulk of the development using whichever platform and combination of tools you're most comfortable with, but recompile the source code and perform a quick functional test of the game in the remaining platforms at least once every day in order to catch any issues early.

- Fix any bugs as soon as they come up, as you never know which kind of other issues will develop down the line as a result of leaving a problem unfixed.

- Don't be afraid to contact publishers via e-mail. You never know which kind of opportunities might develop afterwards.

Breaking Into The Industry (Late May 2009 - Early 2010)

After the experience of releasing Flip Disc, I resumed my work on SPM. I also decided that, since I was already developing the game using a multi-platform library, I might as well target desktop platforms too. The artist that had made the assets for the space complex the year before did a second pass on them and also reworked the various UI widgets to make them more modern.

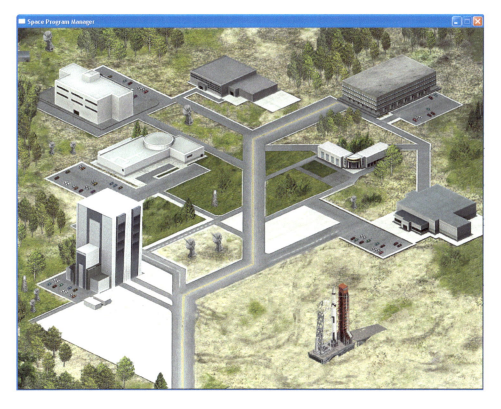

-The second iteration of the space complex (circa mid-2009).-

In May 2009, I was approached by the owner of a local video game company, whom I had met some years earlier in a local gathering of hobbyist game developers. His company had managed to secure an investment round and was looking for programmers. After some discussions with him, I accepted a full-time job as a Software Developer in a small team that was in charge of porting the Torque 3D engine[4] to the Nintendo Wii platform. This was a very exciting opportunity for me, and I remember being quite excited about the fact that I got the chance to work with the Nintendo Wii development kit!

In August 2009, I passed my last final exam and graduated from college, which left me with lots of spare time to work on the game during the evening. The majority of this time was spent writing tools to automate the conversion and validation of the game's database.

Once I had devoted more time into the SPM prototype, I tried contacting various publishers from Europe and the United States to pitch them the project and show them the work that had gone into it so far. Alas, I got no replies from them. At some point I even showed the C++ prototype to the owner of the company I was working for and asked him if he was interested in providing me with resources in order to finish it. He said he had liked the concept behind the game and proposed a deal where the company would take my concept and develop a game based on it. The only catch was that I wouldn't get any royalties or bonus derived from the project. While I wanted the game to see the light of day, I wasn't very excited about the prospects of giving it away for nothing, so the talks never went beyond that stage.

The end of the year concluded with me speaking to the Dean of the Computer Science Engineering department from the college I had graduated a few months earlier, who informed me of an upcoming opportunity with the college. They were opening a new lab that was going to focus on computer games, graphics, and animation, and that she was looking for full-time employees who would split their workday between the lab and undergraduate courses. This sounded like a great opportunity, and I decided to jump on it before it slipped away.

Showcasing The Prototype On The Web (Early 2010)

Before starting my new job, I spent a few weeks of intense work polishing the prototype and integrating a new series of UI assets. I then went on and shared some screenshots in the "Image of the Day" column from gamedev.net. Unfortunately, the thread doesn't seem to be available online anymore, but I recall I got very encouraging feedback from other members of the community.

From a graphical point of view, the new UI looked better than the previous iteration, mostly because we were no longer restricted to color-keyed images and started using images with an alpha channel instead. That being said, the UI design itself was far from optimal from a usability point of view and, looking at the screenshots, one could easily tell that the new desktop screens are just an extended version of the VGA ones which only made the game look poorly planned.

-The second iteration of the UI; Program Categories list (circa early 2010).-

-The second iteration of the UI; Instructions screen (circa early 2010).-

-The second iteration of the UI; Mission Outcome screen (circa early 2010).-

Potential Collaboration With a Polish Company (2010)

In March 2010, I got an e-mail from the owner of a Polish game company who had seen my post in the gamedev.net forums and wanted to talk about SPM with me. We signed an NDA and exchanged a series of e-mails for several months discussing improvements for the game and a potential partnership. He was busy with other ongoing projects, so the rate of communication was a bit slow. Even though I saw some potential in the partnership, I wasn't very sure whether this partnership could provide the time and resources I needed for such a complex game as SPM.

At the end of the year, I met a friend who works in EA Vancouver and told him about my situation. He wisely advised me to start looking for local partners instead, as liaising with a small company located on the other side of the world might prove to be very challenging. I took his advice, parted ways with the Polish company (luckily we never went further than a signed NDA) and began looking for local partners.

• • •

References:
1. http://slitherine.com/games/BA_SPM_Pc
2. http://store.steampowered.com/app/308270
3. https://www.youtube.com/watch?v=JCX1pMzMiZk
4. http://www.garagegames.com/products/torque-3d

PART II [2011 UNTIL 2013]

Looking For Local Partners (First half of 2011)

Following the advice, I was given at the end of 2010, I started looking for local partners to assemble a team and finish the development of the game. I didn't have any money to offer in advance, but at least, I had a playable prototype and a set of requirements, which at least gave me some credibility and didn't turn me into some random guy with a game idea looking for people to implement it for him.

I didn't keep track of the exact number of people I talked to during this period, but it was well over a dozen. I tried local online forums, former colleagues from the game company I worked for during 2009, acquaintances from those former colleagues, and so on. Their answers ranged from "not interested" to "very interested", with various shades of grey in the middle. To be fair, SPM was a risky proposal: no upfront payments, a very ambitious project targeted to a very niche potential market and no guarantees that it would be a financial success.

It was around this time when I partnered with Mauricio Sanjurjo, who would end up producing the dozens of 3D models and the hundreds of renders used in the mission animations of SPM. He used to work in the computer lab from my University and I met him the year before when we worked together on an animation project involving motion capture. He really liked the concept behind SPM and, despite the fact that it was a risky proposition, he decided to jump on board, probably because he realised I was serious about the whole project.

Mauricio started by going through the existing 3D models and "cleaning them up" by tweaking their meshes and enhancing their materials. I continued making progress in the programming, the expansion of the game database and the creation of the various text assets.

Crossing The Pond (Second half of 2011)

Around Easter of 2011, I managed to get a full-time job as a Software Engineer at an aviation company based in Bournemouth, a town located on the southwest coast of the UK. I had never been to Europe (or even outside America) before, so there was no doubt this was going to be a unique experience! After sorting out the paperwork required to move here, I emigrated to the UK in August 2011. I told Mauricio that, despite this big change for me, I was still committed to SPM and that I would make the most out of this opportunity by trying to find a publisher for the game.

The adaptation process to the new country went very smoothly and, within weeks, I was already resuming my work on SPM during the evenings. I also quickly became used to the comfort of ordering used books on the subject of space exploration from Amazon and getting them delivered to my door. I couldn't do that before coming to the UK because very few sellers (if any) would dispatch used books to my native Argentina, so I was really glad about finally being able to read material that was unavailable to me before.

Around this time, I was already planning to contact Slitherine Ltd, a publisher based in Epsom, UK, though I was waiting until we had something more substantial to show. More specifically, we were waiting for a 2D/UI artist who had joined us earlier that year to have some preliminary work ready on the new UI system so that we could pitch a stronger proposal and have better chances of them getting back to us. Unfortunately, that preliminary work never materialised and the artist ended up abandoning the project in early 2012. A few weeks before he left us, though, I had already made up my mind that I was going to contact Slitherine anyway, show them what we have and see how things panned out. This turned out to be the right decision.

Publishing Deal With Slitherine (Q1 2012)

According to my e-mail records, I sent an e-mail pitch to Slitherine on December 25th, 2011, which sounds about right, since the UK comes to an absolute halt on that particular day of the year and I probably didn't have anything else to do!

Slitherine is a medium-sized publisher that focuses on strategy games, mostly wargames, with a strong historical flavour. Many games from their catalogue are based on World War II, though there's a healthy dose of games from other eras such as the Civil War, the Trojan Wars and even some sci-fi and fantasy titles in there as well. Although they didn't have any games based on the subject of space exploration, the fact that they favoured titles based on historical events made SPM a welcome addition.

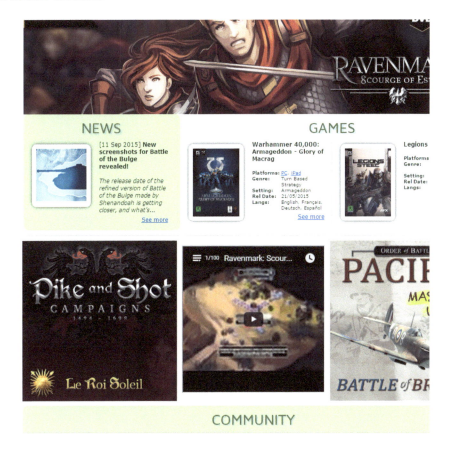

-Slitherine's webpage at the time of this writing.-

As a publisher, Slitherine works mostly with small and medium-sized developers. Some of them are full-time developers, whereas others are people with a day job who work on their own games during the evenings and weekends. They also have to their credit several success stories of developers who, after their first hit, turned their part-time game development efforts into full-time endeavours.

Slitherine initially started as a developer around 2000, but then switched the focus to game publishing, and keeping their internal development to one or two simultaneous projects. Lately, they have gone even further in that direction and are focusing most of their resources on helping the developers that work with them by providing them the tools and support they need to be successful. In 2010, they acquired Matrix Games, a publisher from the US with a very similar background. In late 2012 they acquired Ageod, another developer and publisher of strategy games. Slitherine, Matrix Games, and Ageod are collectively known as the Slitherine Group.

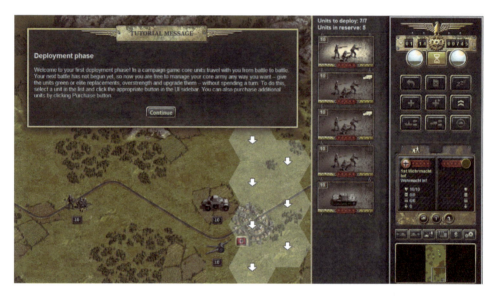

-Panzer Corps, one of Slitherine's most successful titles.-

I got a reply from one of Slitherine's owners in early January, who told me they were quite interested in our project. We went ahead and signed the mandatory NDA (Non-Disclosure Agreement) and began exchanging dozens of e-mails to arrange the details of a publishing agreement. They were very responsive at all times, and diligently answered all the questions I had regarding the extensive publishing agreement document. Before signing the contract, I told them I wanted to meet them in person. So they drove all the way down to Bournemouth (a 2+ hour journey) during a cold February evening to have a chat with me. They brought the boxes from some of their games to the meeting and discussed their latest releases with me. This was all very positive and encouraging, and it confirmed my thoughts that SPM, due to its historical nature, was a good fit to their existing catalogue. Moreover, the fact that they were a small publishing house and that the owners were very hands-on and actively engaged in the day to day issues was very reassuring for me, as it gave me the impression that they would genuinely care about the game doing well.

The only thing that worried them about SPM was the fact that it lacked a competitive aspect to it. They were concerned that their fan base would dismiss it as it was more of a "software toy"[5] and not a game with a clear conflict and an opponent to beat. I understood their concerns, as the lack of a competitive aspect was something that I had taken into account four years earlier. But the reality is that I didn't have the resources to create all the required assets to support more than one faction on a game that would span the dawn of the space age all the way to a manned mission to Mars. The competitive aspect would have to wait until Space Program Manager 2.

Changing Horses: Switching to Unity and C# (Q1 2012)

One of the first questions Slitherine's owners asked me when we started the discussion on SPM was whether the game could easily be ported to iPad. They had experienced some early successes in the platform and were confident that the game will do well for portable devices too. The C++ prototype running at a fixed 1024x768 resolution we had at that point was powered by the EDGELIB library, which had support for iOS. I already had the experience of making a multi-platform game using the library, so it was definitely possible. That being said, when I tried running the prototype in full-screen mode on my laptop, the game crashed to desktop. I contacted EDGELIB's support team, but unfortunately, they were unable to provide a solution to my problem. Moreover, I was informed that "EDGELIB does not support 1366x768, for sure", with 1366x768 being the maximum resolution supported by my laptop. Since I knew that SPM would have to support multiple resolutions to be a competitive product, I realised that I might have to ditch EDGELIB and start looking for a new solution.

I had found out about Unity around 2008 though at the time it was impossible for me to get my hands on it since it ran on Mac only, and Mac computers were prohibitively expensive in my country. Nonetheless, I always kept an eye on it and, just like thousands of hobbyist game developers around the world, was elated when it was released for the Windows platform in 2009, and even more so when the Indie version was made available for free a few months later. I had played around with Unity in 2009 and 2010, so I was already moderately familiar with the tool.

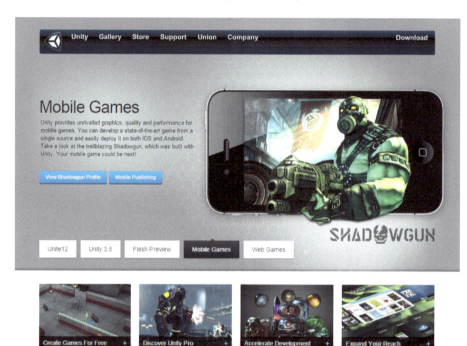

-Unity's webpage, circa March 2012 (retrieved using the Wayback Machine).-

The only thing holding me back from making the move was the fact that applications made in Unity are meant to be written in C#, UnityScript or a variant of Python named Boo. It does have support for C++ plug-ins, though. However, this is not the most convenient method to write a game or application using the engine.

After having spent so many years writing SPM in C++, I was hesitant to throw all that work away. In the end, I decided to bite the bullet and convert the code to C#. I didn't keep track of the exact number of hours it took me to do the conversion, but I recall it was a very fun experience and that it was a lot less effort than I originally anticipated, mostly due to how similar the C# and C++ syntaxes are.

By the end of March, all the core logic was running inside Unity 3, and we would only use C++ to maintain some of the existing validation and scripts conversion tools, which were already bug-free. We would use C# and the .NET libraries for any new tools, though, since they provide excellent support for XML.

The Production Begins (Q2 2012)

By the end of March, the production of SPM was at full steam. We hired an artist from my native Argentina, who was in charge of redesigning the UI and creating the various 2D assets required by the game. Mauricio was creating lots of new 3D models and assembling them into scenes to produce the set of static renders that were going to be used to display the progress of the various space missions. The plan was to produce a considerable number of renders and show them using simple animation effects, such as panning and zooming, to make the sequence more exciting.

We had a rough idea of the game we wanted to make, but we didn't have a complete list of required assets, as we were making things as we went along. To be honest, I wasn't an experienced game designer either, so it would have been next to impossible for me to plan everything in advance, as I didn't know what I didn't know.

-One of the early renders done by Mauricio, our 3D artist: The Mercury-Redstone sitting on the launch pad.-

All the team members were working on SPM on a part-time basis, and I'd arrange separate Skype calls with the rest of the team throughout the week to define tasks, discuss the progress and give them feedback. We were all working on this project on a royalty-based scheme, so it was in everyone's interest for the project to do well, because the amount of money they would end up getting was directly linked to that.

I cannot disclose the actual figures of the compensation, but suffice it to say that all the team members got a significant fraction of the revenue pie. I was advised multiple times that I shouldn't be so generous regarding the revenue share, but I thought (and still think) it was the right thing to do. These developers would be putting an incredible amount of hours into a project, with no upfront payment whatsoever and a loosely defined objective, as there wasn't a full list of assets that needed to be produced. In my view, this kind of commitment should be suitably rewarded. While it's true that I had already invested quite heavily in the game, both in terms of time and money, compensating them properly was my way of saying "Thank you" and acknowledging the fact that they were risking a lot to build this game that I wanted to make.

-Another of the early renders; The Titan II booster with a Gemini spacecraft mounted on top.-

Going back to the development, it was at this stage when we started discussing ideas with the 2D artist on how we were going to approach the UI. Our first solution involved rendering the space complex as a series of sliding panels above that will come in and out of the screen. While visually appealing, we realised this solution wasn't going to work well for those game screens that needed to display an enormous amount of information. Also, the sliding effect was neat during the first couple of minutes, but after that it became annoying. So we ended up discarding this solution altogether and adopted a full-screen approach instead.

-First approach to the UI, which involved the use of sliding panels.-

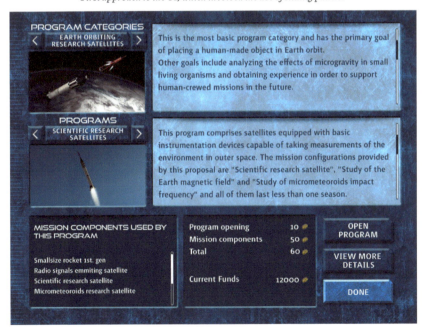

-The visual style for the first era of the game (early manned programs such as Project Mercury).-

The game was going to span various eras of space exploration history (i.e., the early stages of Mercury, Gemini and Apollo, the Space Shuttle, the ISS and the manned mission to Mars). We did some tests to provide a different visual style for each era which, we thought, would give a nice touch to the game while also providing the player with a sense of progression. To do this, we used references from each one of those eras, such as pictures and documents from NASA.

-The visual style for the second era of the game (manned programs that preceded the Moon missions, such as Gemini).-

-The visual style for the third era of the game (the Lunar programs, such as Apollo).-

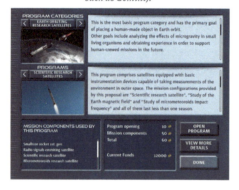

-The visual style for the fourth era of the game (the International Space Station).-

-The visual style for the fifth era of the game (the manned Mission to Mars).-

Again, after doing some tests, we found out that this idea didn't work so well in practice either, so we decided to use a unified style across the whole game. It was also around this time that we realised that Unity's GUI system wasn't a good fit for our game, so I "shopped around" Unity's Asset Store to find a replacement. During my search, I came across NGUI, a library developed by a single programmer which had very positive review scores and was regularly updated. It also just so happened to be 50% off. Thus, I decided to give it a go.

Unity released an entirely new UI system at the end of 2014. The new UI system is great, and it's the one we're using for our current game projects, but I am certainly grateful for coming across NGUI back in 2012 and deciding to adopt it. This was an excellent decision, and using NGUI certainly made our lives easier during the development process.

Bringing Buzz Aldrin On Board and Managing The Team (Q3 - Q4 2012)

The second half of 2012 brought many exciting events, one of the most important being that we managed to get Buzz Aldrin's blessing in order to use his name in our game. Appropriately enough, the game went from being called "Space Program Manager" to "Buzz Aldrin's Space Program Manager".

Buzz Aldrin is a former United States Air Force military pilot and NASA astronaut. He was the "Lunar Module Pilot" (LMP) in the Apollo 11 mission, which took place in July 1969 and was the first one to successfully achieve a manned landing on the surface of the Moon. Along with Neil Armstrong, who passed away in August 2012, they were the first human beings to walk on another celestial body. Shortly after the Apollo 11 mission ended, he retired from both NASA and the Air Force and has been a strong advocate for establishing a permanent human presence on Mars. He has written many fiction and non-fiction books and frequently travels around the world to deliver public speeches and presentations.

How did we manage to obtain his permission to use his name in the game? It all started nearly a year and a half earlier, in March 2011, some weeks before I applied to the Software Engineer role in the UK. I contacted Buzz's representatives via the contact form of their webpage (www.buzzaldrin.com), showed them the work we had done so far but, after exchanging some e-mails with them, they politely declined to go ahead with the project. To be fair, it was a very bold move from me, and the fact that I even got a reply to my original enquiry was more than enough to make me happy.

After we had signed the development agreement with Slitherine in March 2012, I suggested that they contact Buzz's representatives again. The communications between Slitherine's Marketing Team and Buzz's representatives spread throughout months and, finally, in early August 2012, we arranged a meeting with him and Christina, his Mission Control Director, in the hotel they were staying in central London. They were spending a few days there to make some public appearances in the context of the Olympic Games, so it was a great opportunity for us to meet them in person. I had never met an astronaut in person before, and the first one was the "Lunar Module Pilot" from the Apollo 11 mission, what an honour!

The meeting went very well and stretched on for nearly three hours. During the event, we listened to Buzz's views regarding the optimal way to get to Mars, discussed the current state of affairs in space exploration and showed him some of our work, mostly the 3D renders that our artist Mauricio had been working on. He was very impressed by the quality of the renders and asked us to create a representation of a very interesting concept devised by him in the mid-1980s called the "Aldrin Mars Cycler" or simply "Mars Cycler".

In a nutshell, the Mars Cycler concept is a system that makes a clever use of orbital mechanics and allows a spacecraft to "cycle" perpetually between the Earth and Mars. This approach considerably reduces the costs of establishing a permanent presence on Mars. It's a very interesting idea, and I encourage you to learn more about it by visiting the articles area[6] on Buzz's personal webpage.

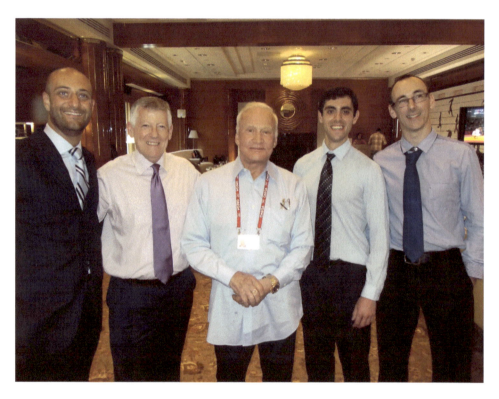

-First meeting with Buzz Aldrin, August 2012. From left to right: Marco Minoli (Slitherine's Marketing Director), JD McNeil (Slitherine's Chairman), Buzz Aldrin, Ignacio Liverotti and Iain McNeil (Slitherine's Development Director)-

Needless to say, both Mauricio and I were extremely excited about the request, and for a couple of weeks, he pretty much stopped creating 3D models and renders for the game and focused entirely on creating a short animation of the Mars Cycler approaching the Red Planet. I did my part by exchanging e-mails with Buzz and his team to refine the requirements and nail down the details of the representation of the vehicle. This also involved a two-hour call with Buzz himself on Skype from my living room in Bournemouth to his place in California (how neat is that!).

The result of this effort, with Mauricio doing most of the grunt work, is a twenty-second hi-res animation featuring a 360° orbit around a representation of the Aldrin Cycler approaching Mars. Both Mauricio and I were very satisfied with the results and are very proud about the fact that our work is featured in Buzz's webpage and that he uses the animation we made for him in some of his public presentations.

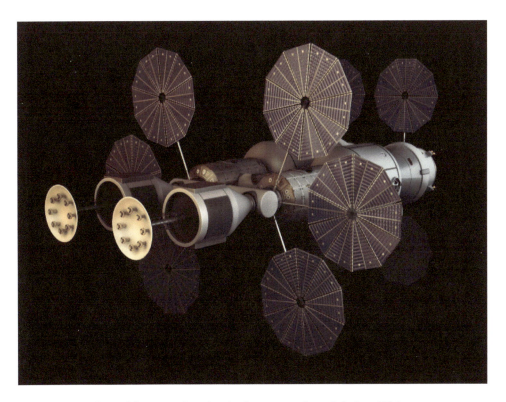

-A frame of the Mars Cycler animation that our 3D artist made for Buzz Aldrin.-

We held yet another meeting with Buzz and his Mission Control Director, Christina, in October, where we finally wrapped up the details of the collaboration, which was finally announced in mid-December 2012. The announcement was very brief, and it focused mostly on the fact that Slitherine had partnered with Buzz Aldrin, and that a game was in development as a result of this partnership. Neither the name of the game nor many details about it were revealed, but it generated a very positive response from the community, who was very happy to learn that a game based on space exploration was in development.

-*The announcement of the collaboration between Buzz and Slitherine (December 2012).*-

While there were some very exciting events going on in certain areas of the project, on the development side this was probably one of the timeframes that I remember less fondly. I won't go too much into the details, but suffice to say that we were experiencing lots of problems in the 2D/UI department. The artist wasn't able to come up with an appealing visual style for the game and would always deliver a slightly modified version of the screens we already had from the C++ prototype. We also experienced communication problems, as some of the hard questions I'd ask him via e-mail would remain unanswered.

New 2D/UI Artist and Announcements (Q1 2013)

In early January 2013, we hired Boris, an artist from Vancouver, to fill the 2D/UI role. He had a background in AAA game studios (Electronic Arts and Activision) and was already familiar with designing user interfaces for management games, so he was a great fit for SPM. At that time, he was working from home so, despite there being a time difference of eight hours between West Canada and the UK, this worked out just fine for us. I'd call him on Skype after coming back from work at around 5.30 PM (that would be 9.30 AM in Vancouver) and we'd discuss the game for a couple of hours. Then he'd set out to start producing mock-up screens and concepts based on the results of our discussions so that we could review them at the next meeting the following day. Rinse and repeat.

Boris started by creating diagrams to get a clear picture of how the various parts of the game fitted together. I was completely willing to get rid of the existing UI code and redo it if that's what it took to produce a better game. Luckily we had a very clear separation between the classes that dealt with the game database and the ones that handled the UI logic, so it was just a matter of rethinking the layout of the screens and the way players would interact with them, and then writing the code for it. The core logic classes, such as **ProgramsManager** and **MissionComponentsManager** (which started as C++ classes and were then converted to C#), would stay the same.

We spent roughly one month working on the UI redesign, just in time to have something ready to show during the public announcement of the game, which happened in mid-February 2013. The announcement was covered by popular gaming news websites including Rock, Paper, Shotgun and The Escapist. The announcement got its own thread on the Slitherine's forums, and we got some very interesting initial feedback from their already established fan base in <u>this thread.</u>[7]

A quick glance at the posts from the previous thread reveals that the announcement of the game was well received by the community. However, it also confirmed a fact that had already been considered during the inception phase of the game; it lacked a competitive aspect. Sure, it was nice to get the chance to play with historical space hardware such as Sputnik and Apollo. But it wasn't entirely appealing to some members of the community, who were looking for clear objectives and a concrete opponent to beat.

I acknowledged this feedback but, in the same way, I had done a year earlier during my first meeting with Slitherine, I had to disregard it since it would have

Manage To Mars: Buzz Aldrin's Space Program Manager

By Jim Rossignol on February 8th, 2013 at 11:00 am.

Creepily-named publisher Slitherine send word that they're going to be launching a space-project management game with Buzz Aldrin's name on it later this year (and his advice was sought in researching the development, apparently). In **Buzz Aldrin's Space Program Manager** you will be tasked with a sandbox management scenario in which you must train astronauts and their support staff, while at the same time doing R&D and dealing with politicians. It's going to be heavy on the realism, of course, but there's scope for fantasy too: "Develop the X-15 Space plane, the Sputnik satellite, the Mercury, Gemini and Apollo manned spacecrafts and in later episodes on to Mars! You are not limited to the missions that did launch – you can also try out many that were planned but that never left the drawing board. For example, instead of sending men to the Moon using the Lunar Orbit Rendezvous (LOR) approach used by Project Apollo in the late 1960s and early 1970s, you will be able to rewrite history and use either the alternative Earth Orbit Rendezvous (EOR) or Direct Ascent schemes."

So basically giving us the space history we *should* have had. Sigh.

-Coverage of the announcement of SPM in Rock, Paper, Shotgun (February 2013).-

required a considerable amount of resources. Resources we simply didn't have. If things with Space Program Manager went well, we could always release a "Race to the Moon and Beyond" module later.

It's also important to mention that, by this stage, we already knew that Space Program Manager was going to be released in three instalments. The first one would cover from the dawn of the space age up to the Lunar Landings, the second one would cover the establishment of a permanent presence in Earth orbit via space stations and the third one would cover a manned mission to Mars. We had made the decision around mid-2012, when we realised that aiming for a single, massive release, would be too big of a challenge for us on various fronts (historical information to research, amount of graphical content and data to produce, game balancing, etc.)

The press release mentioned that the game was expected to be done in June 2013, which was a goal I knew was completely unrealistic- I had brought a new artist a mere five weeks ago and I was working a full-time job that only allowed me to work on the game during the evenings and weekends. There were so many unknowns that, to me, hitting a release date of June simply wasn't going to happen. Still, the publisher wanted to specify a release date in the announcement and, despite my objections, they went ahead for June, stating that missing the release date wouldn't be such a big deal anyway. In hindsight, I think I should have put my foot down and refuse to commit to a release date, as I knew we were not going to make it and it was going to reduce our public image for no apparent benefit.

After the announcement, we spent another month or so working on the UI and then we started working in parallel on the mission animations. Since Boris would be working on the game full-time, we decided to raise the quality bar a bit more and display the missions as a series of layered animations. This still wouldn't match the level of quality that we would get by doing full 3D animations (a prohibitively costly endeavour), but it would certainly be a lot less dull than showcasing a series of static renders sporting basic effects such as panning and zooming. The final results look quite neat for a game with such a small budget, but I'll let you be the judge[8].

If you're interested in the details behind the animations and all the process behind their creation, I encourage you to read an article[9] which was published weeks before the Early Access Program started in late October 2013.

The Data and Text Scripts

By this stage, our internal development processes and tools were already in place and, except for some minor changes during the Early Access Program the following year, they would remain virtually unmodified throughout the rest of the development process. In this section, we'll cover some of the most important aspects, including some simple techniques we used in order to keep the game as bug-free as possible.

Internally, the game data is stored as a set of XML files. I'm a big fan of XML due to a variety of reasons: it's text-based, human-readable, and there are plenty

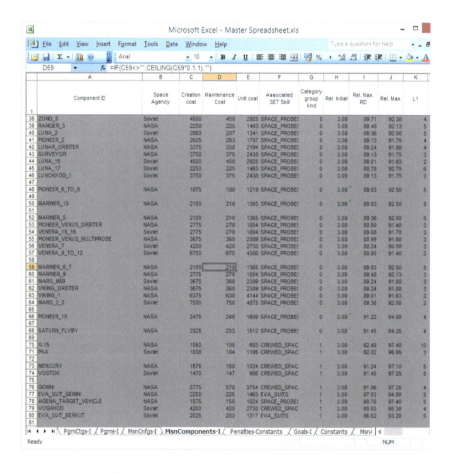

-The Mission Components page from the Master Spreadsheet.-

of libraries out there in order to read and process these kind of files. I decided to adopt the XML format early on in the development process by using a library called irrXML, which was developed by the same author of the Irrlicht engine. The usage of XML survived throughout the whole project, even after moving to different engines (from Irrlicht, then EDGELIB and finally Unity) and even programming languages (from C++ to C#).

In spite of the convenience of working with XML files, the game database is actually stored in an Excel spreadsheet named MasterSpreadsheet.xls. The spreadsheet has a variety of pages, one for each type of entities groups from the game (i.e., "Program Categories", "Programs", "Mission Configurations" and "Mission Components").

To get the information from the Excel spreadsheet into the game, we convert each individual page into a CSV file and run a series of console applications

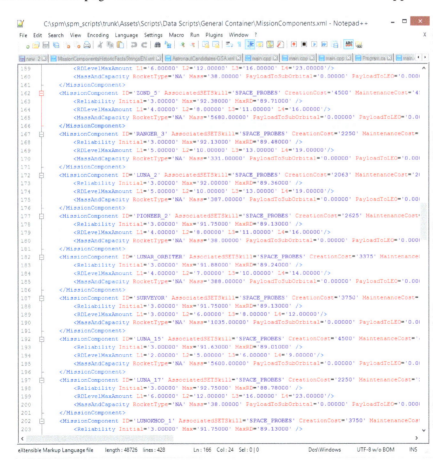

-The Mission Components XML data file that is fed into the game engine.-

written in C++ and C# that produce the final XML files. According to my records, the first one of these tools was written in early 2009, although after we had made the switch to Unity and C#, I found that the support provided by the .Net libraries were a lot more convenient, so all tools written after 2012 were developed in C#. None of the C++ tools were rewritten, as they were already working and it didn't make sense to spend time on that.

Someone once asked me why I didn't use a lightweight embedded database such as SQLite to store the game data. An embedded relational database certainly has its advantages, but I've found that the approach of using an Excel spreadsheet is lot more convenient:

- It's very easy to visualise a significant amount of data on the screen at once.

- Relationships can be quickly established between fields from different entities. If you change the ID for a given goal in the Goals-I page and the change will be immediately reflected in the relevant goal dependencies column in the MsnCnfgs-I page. Alter the value of a single cell in the Constants page to increase the unit cost of all rockets by 20%, and so on.

After using the various conversion tools to generate the various XML files, a series of validation tools were used in order to ensure database consistency. All these tools, along with the Master Spreadsheet, grew organically throughout the development process as we added new game rules and mechanics. Validation tools will check, for example, that the script for a given mission actually includes all the goal IDs that are meant to be achieved by completing said mission. We also have tools to check that XML files are well-formed, that text scripts don't contain any extraneous characters that might freak out the XML parser and so on.

Many bug reports that we got during the development of the game were due to either missing or ill-formed data. For example, a mission data script would use a certain mission component that wasn't defined in the spreadsheet. Every time we got a bug report, I would ask for a save file so that I could reproduce it. Most of the time the root of the problem was very easy to identify, and it would involve an issue with a data script. However, instead of just fixing the offending data script, I would extend one of the existing validation tools to catch the problem automatically. If the validation involved accessing a group of scripts and didn't fit neatly in one of the existing tools, I'd start writing a new one as a separate C# program. I'd then run the updated (or brand new) validation tool against the game database and, usually, that would uncover the presence of the exact same issue in several other scripts. This methodology of adding a validation mechanism in order to prevent the occurrence of the same issue really paid off once the final game shipped.

Buzz Aldrin's Space Program Manager (PC)

Available at: Matrix Games store, Steam, Amazon.

Space Sector score:
8.1/10
Great

(about the score system)

The Good:

- Definitely lives up to the predecessor in both feel and game play.
- Easy to pick up and go with, doesn't take long to get a game going.
- The very friendly UI makes learning how to play the game a breeze, while the random factors involved in space flights and crew training keep an enjoyable level of difficulty present.
- The game's simplicity in both function and looks makes it easy enough for a child to get involved, while also maintaining enough depth to interest an adult player.
- Very realistic depictions of both craft and missions makes the game very, very authentic, with a treasure trove of information ready to be read.
- And as sad as it is these days for this to be classed as a positive: I can't find any bugs in game, even after going at it for twelve hours straight and trying my hardest to cause it to glitch out.

The Bad:

- The music can get quite repetitive, especially the Russian space port theme, which is so over the top as to be annoying.
- The multiplayer is of limited use due to how it's set up, making it awkward for quick pick-up games.
- Flights occur way too quickly, reducing the ability for the game to build up any tension like that found in real space launches.
- The AI isn't willing to make many gambles, making overtaking the AI with risky missions fairly easy so long as they don't explode in your face.

-Space Sector's review[10] of the released version of SPM, which praised the absence of bugs.-

Getting Everything Ready for the Early Access Program (Q2 and Q3 2013)

While the whole team kept plugging along with the development of the game, Slitherine disclosed more details about it in their yearly "Home of the Wargamers" event, which in 2013 it took place in the Historicon convention in Fredericksburg, Virginia and gathered various members from the press. Iain McNeil, Slitherine's

Director, kick-started the event showing SPM's official trailer.[11]

He then went on and showcased a video from Buzz[12] himself talking about the game. Buzz was meant to be at the event, but unfortunately, some last minute personal problems prevented him from doing so. In any case, recording the video for us was a nice gesture from him and we were grateful for it.

Iain then proceeded to show some work in progress screenshots, some of them straight from a recent build, and the rest from our mock-up builds, which featured functionality that was soon to be implemented.

-Some of the work in progress shown at the "Home of the Wargamers 2013" event in Historicon.-

Unfortunately, since at that time I had a day job, I wasn't able to attend the event, but from what I was told by Slitherine's Directors, the reception among the press was very positive. The critical feedback points were that they were happy to see a title that departed from the usual "war" subject though they also voiced some concerns about the lack of a competitive aspect. Again, I acknowledged those concerns, but at this point, there was nothing we could do other than being confident that the game as originally envisioned would still do well, and that its success will allow us to create a "Race to the Moon" expansion at a later stage. It was also during this event that Slitherine announced that SPM would launch at the end of October 2013 as an Early Access Program. The Early Access Program wouldn't be conducted on Steam, but on their own online stores at the Slitherine and Matrix Games websites, and it would feature the following three tiers:

- **Mercury:** which included access to the digital version of the game and all the updates delivered until the final release.

- **Gemini:** which included the digital version plus the delivery of a boxed copy of the game once the product got finally released.

- **Apollo:** which included all the contents from the Mercury and Gemini tiers plus the opportunity for players to get their names and pictures featured in the game as an employee of the GSA in their group of choice (i.e., "Flight Controllers", "Scientists, Engineers and Technicians" or "Astronauts").

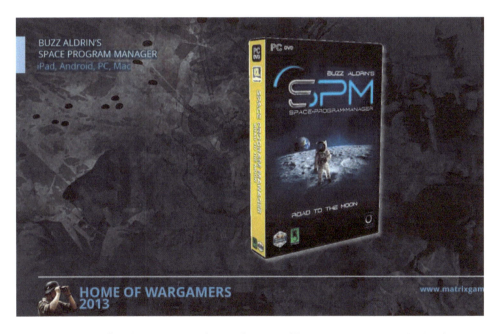

-One of the slides from the presentation of SPM in the "Home of the Wargamers 2013" event in Historicon.-

The announcement was well received. A vocal minority complained about the fact that the game was being released in three paid parts but, fortunately enough, neither Slitherine in the role of publisher, nor myself in the role of Community Manager, had to address those complaints. Various members of the community itself stepped in and backed our decision: the game has a lot of content which is very expensive to produce, so we shouldn't feel sorry for not giving it away for free.

Regarding the decision to go for an Early Access Program, I don't remember the exact date where that decision was made, but I believe it was around June 2013 and that it was suggested by Slitherine's Marketing team. The idea of an Early Access Program was a relatively novel concept in those days, with Minecraft and Kerbal Space Program being one of the first games to adopt this distribution approach. SPM would be Slitherine's first experience conducting an Early Access Program so it would be a learning experience for all of us, and we weren't quite sure on what to expect.

With our spirits high after all the positive response that SPM got in Historicon, we made the final sprint to get everything ready for the launch of the Early Access Program. This involved delivering a build as stable as possible (i.e., no crashes and no serious bugs), while at the same time aiming to get as much content in as we could possibly fit. We knew for sure that we were not going to be able to have all the mission animations ready for the start of the Early Access Program, but we were still planning to ship a considerable number so that players could actually enjoy a decent number of hours of gameplay. The same principle applied to build stability. We knew that the first build would have some bugs in it, but we didn't want the product to feel so unfinished that it would actually end up putting off players, who might end up dismissing the product and never coming back to it.

Launching the Early Access Program (Q4 2013)

The Early Access Program start date was scheduled for October 29th, 2013. That was on a Tuesday and was deliberately planned that way so that we could address any urgent issues before the beginning of the first weekend. The initial version was marked as 0.7.0, not because we had been keeping track of version numbers internally up to that point, but because I thought that 0.7.0 should give us enough room to iterate until the final release of 1.0 which, at the time, we expected to happen roughly two or three months later.

Version 0.7.0 of SPM had already been "locked" and sent to Slitherine roughly a week earlier, and they would take care of doing some general testing, creating the installer, uploading it to their online stores and so on. It was also very encouraging to see players opening a thread in the forums[13] asking at which exact time the game was going to be available for purchase later that day, and showing their overall enthusiasm for the release

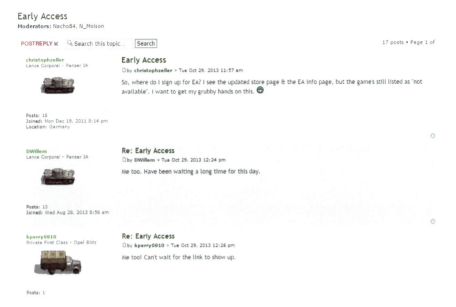

POSTREPLY ⤆   🔍 Search this topic...   Search   17 posts • Page 1 of

christophzeller
Lance Corporal - Panzer IA

Early Access
⬜ by **christophzeller** » Tue Oct 29, 2013 11:57 am

So, where do I sign up for EA? I see the updated store page & the EA info page, but the game's still listed as "not available". I want to get my grubby hands on this. 😬

Posts: 18
Joined: Mon Dec 19, 2011 8:14 pm
Location: Germany

DWillem
Lance Corporal - Panzer IA

Re: Early Access
⬜ by **DWillem** » Tue Oct 29, 2013 12:24 pm

Me too. Have been waiting a long time for this day.

Posts: 13
Joined: Wed Aug 28, 2013 8:56 am

kperry0910
Private First Class - Opel Blitz

Re: Early Access
⬜ by **kperry0910** » Tue Oct 29, 2013 12:26 pm

Me too! Can't wait for the link to show up.

Posts: 1

-A thread in the Slitherine forums opened by members of the community on the starting date of the Early Access Program.-

The initial number of sales was modest but promising, especially taking into account that SPM is a product that only appeals to a small niche and that Polar Motion was a virtually unknown developer. The overall initial response from the community was encouraging and, even though the game wasn't finished, they were certainly enjoying what we had managed to deliver on day one. We got some bug reports within the first 24 hours, the biggest problem being that the animations for certain missions were crashing. I tracked the issue down and found out that some data files were corrupted, so we proceeded to rebuild them and, along with some other fixes and improvements, we released SPM version 0.7.3 on November 1st, 2013, three days after the start date of the Early Access Program. From that moment onwards, we started releasing weekly updates every single Friday until mid-January 2014, even on Christmas week. Each update included a combination of bug-fixes, new gameplay mechanics and content, and players were very happy to see the game undergoing significant changes on a regular basis.

One of the reasons I believe it was so easy for us to release updates on a weekly basis was because I was the only programmer on the project. Every time a new bug report came in (usually with an attached save file), I could quickly reproduce the problem and fix it. We would obviously keep getting more bug reports across the Early Access Program, but by improving our internal tools we could be sure that we won't go through the embarrassment of fixing the same type of problem again! Moreover, if I wanted to add a new feature to the game, or change the way something works, the only person that I'd need to agree with was myself, so it was very straightforward. The downside is that I didn't have anyone looking over my shoulder and warn me if I was doing something silly and getting into a rabbit hole.

The Decision to go Full-Time (Late 2013)

At the end of November 2013, I visited Slitherine's offices in Epsom. This was my first visit after the Early Access Program started. Slitherine's Directors were very pleased with the initial sales which, while not Earth-shattering, certainly looked promising. Seeing how invested the team members were in the project and the fact that a very enthusiastic community had gathered around it, they offered to finance the rest of the development process and pay me monthly advances so that I could quit my day job and focus 100% on the development of the game. The rest of the developers would still be working part-time on the project, but I would get the chance to focus on it entirely. A much-needed change, since combining the development of SPM with my day job had proven to be very straining!

It was also during this meeting that we started evaluating the possibility to raise the bet and address the most important request we were getting from the community: the lack of a competitive aspect. The community wanted to play an updated version of the original "Buzz Aldrin's Race into Space", they wanted to play as either NASA or the Soviets in a race to be the first to the Moon (and then on to Mars). Adding the "Race to the Moon" to SPM wasn't a decision to be taken lightly, as it had many potential consequences:

- **A significant amount of additional development effort.** - Not only would extra work come from the programming side (i.e., ripping the existing codebase apart), but also on the content creation side (3D models for the Soviet hardware, renders, the creation of the mission animations, text files, etc.)

- **Delaying the final release date.** We had originally planned for an Early Access Program that would take roughly three months. Even though players would be getting a lot more for free, the truth is that the final version won't be delivered as early as originally promised and this may, or may not, upset some members of the community.

- **Developer burn-out.** This issue was raised by one of Slitherine's Directors. Despite the fact that he really wanted the game to get a "Race to the Moon" campaign, he was genuinely worried that this extra push would have an adverse impact on the development team, who had already been burning the midnight oil for months up to this point.

All these were very valid points and, even though I was eager to extend the scope of the project and had no issues with ripping the codebase apart to fit the new functionality. I still had to convince the rest of the developers, since they were the ones who would have to create the audio and visuals in order to support the "Race to the Moon" campaign.

I spoke with the rest of the team after my visit to Slitherine and, to be honest, I didn't even have to persuade them about the additions. They agreed that most members of the community wanted a "Race to the Moon" campaign badly and that the lack of it was probably already costing us a lot. We all agreed it was going to be a big undertaking and, to be honest, we were a bit exhausted after all the effort we had already put in up to that point, but we were also confident that the extra work would pay off in the end.

I proceeded to hand in my resignation notice for my day job. December 31st, 2013 would be my last official date there so, starting on January 1st, 2014, I was going to be working full time on the game. Mauricio, the 3D artist, joked about this and told me that the situation was analogous to "quitting your day job and becoming a full-time mum to take care of your new-born baby". I cannot say I disagree with this analogy.

• • •

References:

5. https://en.wikipedia.org/wiki/Non-game
6. http://buzzaldrin.com/space-vision/rocket_science/aldrin-mars-cycler/
7. http://www.slitherine.com/forum/viewtopic.php?t=40768
8. https://www.youtube.com/watch?v=vpTibwtzk0g
9. http://www.slitherine.com/forum/viewtopic.php?f=58&t=45277
10. http://www.spacesector.com/blog/2014/11/buzz-aldrins-space-program-manager-road-to-the-moon-review/
11. https://www.youtube.com/watch?v=dSJmQkeI9ho
12. https://www.youtube.com/watch?v=anqGd6Vgn2Q
13. http://www.slitherine.com/forum/viewtopic.php?f=226&t=45703

PART III [2014 AND 2015]

Full-Time Mode (January - March 2014)

The first days after switching to full-time work on the project were great in terms of productivity. One might naively assume that, for example, if you are working on average three hours per day on a given project and suddenly switch to nine hours a day, your output should roughly triple. What I found out is that the output goes well above that due to a number of reasons:

- Your mind becomes less cluttered, and all the expensive context switching that comes from juggling a day job with the project goes away.

- For those evenings when you are "in the zone", you can carry on working for a couple extra -and usually extremely productive- hours without worrying about your schedule and the fact that you need to go to bed to get up early the following day.

- You start making a lot more progress in a shorter amount of time. A task that previously would have had to be spread across four or five days of part-time work can now be completed in a single workday. This reduces the overall anxiety and gets you in a virtuous cycle where you realise all the things that are being accomplished, which gets you even more motivated.

As mentioned in a previous chapter, in late November 2013 Slitherine and the development team decided we were going to significantly extend the scope of the project. However, we agreed it was better to keep our decision under wraps and unveil it sometime in mid-January so that it didn't get lost in the holiday season. The announcement was made via a press release on January 13th, 2014. In a nutshell, it said that we had been evaluating all the feedback we got during the first weeks of the Early Access Program and had decided to change the development roadmap. The three most important changes were:

- **A "Race to the Moon" campaign:** This was obviously the biggest one. Players had been asking for this feature ever since the game had been announced, and it was an extremely welcome addition to the roadmap, as they would now be able to lead either NASA or the Soviet Space Agency in order to be the first to achieve a manned lunar landing.

- **A "mix-and-match" gameplay mechanic in order to combine boosters and payloads:** This might not sound like a big deal, but it was a major change that opened up lots of possibilities from a gameplay point of view. It also required the production of a significant amount of assets and changes in the codebase and the user interface.

- **Multiplayer via PBEM:** Now that we were adding a "Race to the Moon" campaign, it only made sense to allow players to compete against each other in order to be the first on the Moon. Slitherine already had a server infrastructure to conduct turn-based multiplayer matches using a Play by E-Mail (PBEM) system, so we decided to take advantage of it.

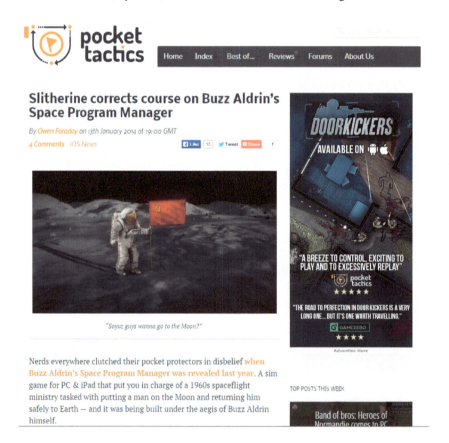

-*Coverage of the announcement of the roadmap changes by popular website Pocket Tactics (link[13]).-*

The announcement was well received by the community and, despite the fact that the final release date had now been effectively pushed back by several months, they understood that this was for the better. The press release didn't include a final release date. Unlike our announcement from early 2013 where missing the expected release date of June wasn't a big deal, this time, the marketing team would invest time and financial resources for the final release, so it was imperative for us to hit the promised date. With so many unknowns, I persuaded Slitherine to wait until we have the foundation and most of the contents for the updated roadmap in place before making us commit to a final release date. Since the project costs were so low anyway, they agreed to my request.

-Community feedback in the Slitherine forums after the roadmap changes announcement.-

The game was already pretty stable by then, so a few days after the announcement we stopped delivering weekly patches and I started ripping the whole codebase apart to create the underlying infrastructure to accommodate the new features. We launched version 0.7.15 at the end of January, followed by a small patch (version 0.7.15.1) in mid-February and we didn't release any new updates until mid-April. In spite of this, I kept monitoring the forums and answering all the questions and feedback left there by the members of the community. I had a self-imposed, unwritten policy of "zero unanswered threads". Although it took a significant amount of time to comply with, I strongly believed it paid off and resulted in an overall better product. I believe this because it forced the developers to stay on top of what the community has to say about the game. That being said, I reckon that this goal might not be achievable for games that manage to form a big community around them, but for SPM, I still think it was the right thing to do.

Version 0.7.16 was released on April 11th. It featured new content, such as Soviet programs with placeholder animations, a brand new random events system (this was suggested by a member of the community in early March, who also contributed a significantly large list of events), a first implementation of the "mix-and-match" functionality and various performance improvements. All in all, a solid update and, more importantly, a good starting point that would allow us to go back to our previous routine of releasing patches on a constant basis.

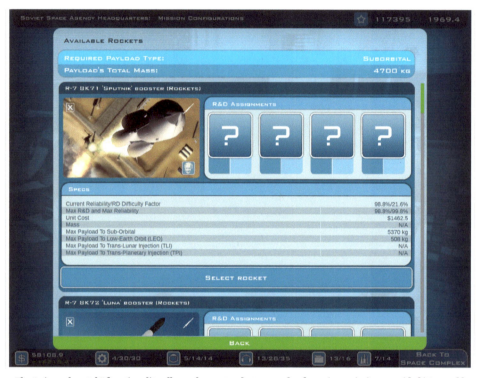

-The "mix-and-match" functionality allows players to select any rocket for a given mission, provided it's capable enough to lift the payload.-

It's important to mention that during the first stages of the Early Access Program, the patching process involved me sending a build to Slitherine every Thursday so that their production team could process it. Which not only involved updating the installers for their online store; but also going through a checklist of test procedures and confirming, among other things, that the game works in various versions of Windows. This ended up being a waste of time for their Production Team, who were already very busy trying to keep up with all the releases from other developers that publish their games through Slitherine. It was also a minor source of frustration for me as well because I wanted to be able to release patches whenever I wanted. In the end, we agreed that testing each and every new

We choose to go to the Moon

update on various versions of Windows wasn't needed, as Unity is very stable when it comes to running on a variety of hardware and operating systems combinations. So I persuaded Slitherine to let me upload patches to their FTP server and ask players to fetch them from there. I couldn't be happier about this new "freedom", as it allowed me to address the issues reported by the community a lot faster.

Another added bonus of the Early Access Program and the community that began forming around it is that I got contacted by several people who were willing to contribute to the game without expecting anything in return. This was something that Slitherine's Directors had already told me it was probably going to happen and, even though I was "prepared" for it, I was still very happy when it actually did. All of these contributors helped us make SPM a much better game, with some of them making huge contributions such as the Buzz-opedia, which is a series of deeply researched articles detailing how the various programs, mission components and mission configurations in the game relate to their real-life counterparts. The articles can be easily accessed from the user interface, and are a real treat for all space buffs that want to know a bit more.

Getting the Full Game Out of the Door

(April - August 2014)

After releasing version 0.7.16 in mid-April, we went back to our routine of releasing frequent updates. In retrospect, the period from April until August 2014 was the most exciting one because it was basically the timeframe when the game went from being a sandbox experience featuring a single fictional space agency into a full game boasting a new campaign mode. The game now boasted more than twice the amount of content, multiplayer support, a revamped UI and lots of tiny gameplay changes that contributed to the overall polishing of the final product.

When conducting an Early Access Program, a developer has already taken payment from their backers and, in my view, has an implicit obligation to provide them with frequent updates. In the case of a major setback or change of plans, it needs to provide even more frequent status updates to keep them in the loop. We had already consistently kept the community in the loop between mid-February and mid-April when we stopped releasing updates due to all the foundation work that needed to be done in order to accommodate the whole new set of features. Now it was the time to start releasing frequent updates again.

One of the biggest challenges of having to release frequent updates is that you need to include something new on each release to keep players engaged and willing to download the latest version and giving it a go. But, at the same time, you need to keep in mind that the clock is still ticking, the final release date is approaching and that you want all your development efforts to effectively contribute in some way or another to the final product. You don't want to spend time on things that won't be part of the final product or, if you do, you want to minimise the time you spend on them. Every day becomes an exercise in evaluating things that need to be done, assigning priorities to them and trying to find ways to schedule them so that you keep producing new things for every new update. At the same time, you team is attempting to do them right the first time so that the updates don't have to be thrown away and redone later.

In early May, Slitherine held their yearly Home of the Wargamers event (HoW '14) in the "Castelo di Pavone". This was an event that brought developers, members of the press and players under the same roof for three days to showcase our work, discuss ideas and have a chat about strategy games.

-Home of the Wargamers '14. From left to right: Ignacio Liverotti, Iain McNeil (Slitherine's Development Director), Alex Shargin (Flashbang Studios) and Marco Minoli (Slitherine's Marketing Director).-

From a personal point of view, HoW '14 was an eye-opener in various fronts. The first one was that I could see other people's reaction to this project we've been working on for such a long time. Until that point, all the feedback I got for SPM was via the forums, but I never had the chance to see people's faces when talking about the game. This was a very refreshing experience and it surely felt encouraging when one member of the press told me "After seeing so many games based on war, it's very exciting to see something different with SPM". Of course, war is a fascinating subject as well and I've played my share of strategy games too in my early teens, but it definitely felt nice to get such encouraging feedback.

The second key takeaway from the whole HoW '14 experience was that it put me in contact with people who were really passionate about playing and analysing computer games. As I mentioned before, I have an interest in playing computer games, but I get a lot more enjoyment out of developing them. I'm not a hard-core gamer and it's extremely unusual for me to find a game where I would log more than 20 hours of playtime (the only exceptions I recall are X-COM in 2013 and, lately, Metal Gear Solid V). Meeting all these members of the press in person and seeing how deep they got into games, how they analysed them and how much they enjoyed digging into their details indeed changed my whole perception on how certain groups of people approach the medium.

After coming back from HoW '14, we released version 0.7.18, which featured a small handful of bug fixes and then spent the following three weeks working on a massive update which included new content, gameplay mechanics and, more importantly, a migration from NGUI 2 to NGUI 3. In mid-July, we issued yet another press release with a new <u>teaser video</u>[14] and announced that we were going to close the Early Access Program in early August and that version 1.0 was going to be released on October 30th and October 31st in our online stores and on Steam, respectively. The release date was now set in stone and, unlike the previous year, this time missing it was going to be a big problem since that would ruin the timing of the marketing and PR campaign built around the game.

-*The press release announcing the release date of SPM version 1.0.*-

Another interesting aspect about this stage is that we decided to hire Nicolas Escats as a full-time contractor for a couple of months. Nicolas is a member of the community who first contacted us at the beginning of the Early Access Program in late 2013. He started by revamping the mission data scripts for the manned programs and doing tons of contributions across various areas. Moreover, he gave us a big hand by sharing with us his profound knowledge of the Soviet space program. I must admit I knew very little about the Soviet space program when we decided to extend the scope of the game. Without his insights about the various flavours of the Soyuz spacecraft, the R-7 booster and the various planned manned lunar mission configurations, the release version of Space Program Manager wouldn't have been nearly as rich and complete.

Final Sprint In Preparation for the PC Release (September - October 2014)

After closing the Early Access Program in mid-August, we began the final sprint to get everything ready for the final release at the end of October. Without a question, this was the most stressful period for both the development team and for Slitherine. The final sprint happened roughly a year ago (it's mid-October 2015 at the time of this writing) and, like it usually happens when one goes through a very intense period, it feels like a black hole in time where one doesn't remember much about it except for a handful of flashes.

During this timeframe, I ramped up the number of work hours to 70+ per week. Long work hours are not sustainable in the long run, but for relatively short periods of time (i.e., a small number of weeks), it's something that can definitely be done. The final release date was already set in stone and it couldn't be moved no matter what, so we had to ensure everything was ready for that day. We could always submit fixes and improvements via post-release updates but, ideally, the game needed to be as polished as it could from day one, as the initial reception has a strong influence on the final shape of the sales curve.

The reason behind the increase in the number of hours was that there were simply so many things to do and loose ends to tie up. The "ninety-ninety" rule states that "The first 90 percent of the code accounts for the first 90 percent of the development time. The remaining 10 percent of the code accounts for the other 90 percent of the development time". In our particular case, we didn't have to cram a second 90% in the last month and a half of development. Yet still, there were lots of things to do; addressing all the incomplete sequences in the mission animations, bug fixes, gameplay balancing, writing the game manual, liaising with the translators, polishing the UI, adding Steam integration, and so on. It was a particularly stressful period for everyone, and I have to thank Slitherine because at some point in late October they noticed that I was really stressed out and suggested that I go to their offices in Epsom for a week so that I didn't have to face the final leg of development on my own.

Around a week before the release date, we finally submitted the "Gold Master" version for PC so that Slitherine could create the various installers, upload them to their online stores and so on. As always, we kept monitoring the various forums during this final sprint. The day before release we posted a message in the forums[15] showcasing some of the improvements done during this stage, which was well received. I also started working on the OSX version, which we were planning to make available a few days after the PC release.

-A screenshot of the revamped version of the Mission Control screen.-

Official Release (Late October - Mid November 2014)

The game was launched on October 30th and October 31st, 2014 in our online stores and on Steam, respectively. We made a "quick tour" video[16] and a last trailer[17] for the launch. Personally, I believe the last trailer is the one that best captures the essence of the game, even if it doesn't show any gameplay footage.

Unfortunately, I'm not allowed to share numbers but, even though the initial sales in our online stores were modest, the numbers on Steam certainly looked a lot better. We got a lot of activity in the Steam forums, mostly from users who hadn't heard about the game before and had only found out about it after the Steam release. I remember spending a huge amount of hours in the forums during the first days after release. Again, I wanted to comply with my unwritten rule of "zero unanswered threads" as much as I could.

The feedback we got from the community was mostly positive though we had some fair criticism about the game's shortcomings, mostly due to the lack of tooltips in the user interface. A very long and interesting thread[18] developed around this subject.

To be fair, the lack of tooltips was something that was mentioned a couple of times during the Early Access Program. This advice went unheeded as we wanted our UI to be compatible with both desktop and touch-based platforms and, at that time, I thought that providing tooltips for the latter wasn't the way to go, as I didn't consider it a clean solution. To me, the icons had to be descriptive enough so that no tooltips were required. Had I got more requests during the Early Access Program, I would have probably reconsidered my decision, but that didn't happen. My suspicion is that at the beginning of the Early Access Program the game mechanics were relatively straightforward, and that since all new mechanics were progressively introduced on every new update, most players learned them gradually. The lesson learned from all this -and that I'll certainly apply in my future games- is that I'll have to keep requesting feedback from people who have never seen the game before all the way until the final release.

The upside of the lengthy discussion in the Steam forums around the lack of tooltips is that it gave us the opportunity to demonstrate how responsive we were in order to address any critical issues. Those who had been with us since the Early Access Program already knew this, but this was the opportunity to show all the newcomers that the development team cared about the project and the players.

Obviously, adding tooltips to the game wasn't going to happen overnight, so our first temporary solution was to quickly create a "UI Reference Guide" in PDF format[19] and make it readily available. The game was already shipping with a lengthy game manual covering the user interface, but this guide provided a handy reference for those that wanted to quickly jump into the game. This responsive attitude earned us some praise from the community[20], which is always encouraging.

The first two weeks of November were as intense as the final sprint before release (retrospectively, I think they can be considered as part of the same sprint!). The result of this effort was SPM 1.1, which was released on November 14th and that included full support for 4:3, 16:9 and 16:10 resolutions, localisation to the German and French languages and tooltips across the entire UI. It also featured improvements to various mission animations and some minor bug fixes. As always, communication is key, so I made sure that the community knew what was going on at all times and when to expect the fixes for all the reported issues by posting in the forums[21].

Releasing SPM 1.1 was a big milestone for us, as it addressed the most pressing problems reported in the original release. There certainly was room for improvement, but, at least, the major issues were now fixed. With that update out of the door, I decided to finally take a couple of days off before resuming work.

Mobile Port and a Big Update
(Mid-November 2014 - Mid-February 2015)

After a very short break, I started working on the mobile port. Originally, we had planned to release SPM concurrently for both desktop and mobile platforms, but then around mid-2014, we decided to focus on desktop platforms only and worry about the rest later. In theory, the development of the mobile port should have been pretty much straightforward, since the game was made in Unity and didn't use any platform-specific functionality. In practice, getting the mobile port to run on iOS devices took a significant amount of time because of a number of technical decisions I made throughout the initial stages of the project.

As you might remember from previous sections, the game depicts the progress of all missions using a system of animated layers, a consequence of the fact that we didn't aim to develop a real-time 3D game due to the high production costs involved. This animation system requires separate assets for each layer and, to store them in a compressed format, they need to be square and their dimensions need to be to the power of two. This is fine for desktop platforms which have, for all intents and purposes, an unlimited amount of disk space, but that's not the case for mobile devices.

Unity 4 provides two distinct ways to store information. The first one is the "resources file", which is a very straightforward method and it's the one that SPM used during its early stages when the total amount of assets was relatively small. In a nutshell, the Unity project needs to have a folder named "Resources" and the engine will grab everything that is located in there and put it inside a single massive file when building the game. Assets inside the file can be easily retrieved using the **Resources.Load** method provided by the Unity API. The only downside is that the resources file has a size limit, and we reached that limit in SPM before the Early Access Program started, so we had to change our approach and adopt a different technique.

The second method, and the one we ended up adopting, is called "asset bundles". In essence, asset bundles are container files that store assets (e.g., models, textures, text scripts, etc.) in a compressed format so that they can be loaded on demand. When loading asset bundles inside a Unity game, there's an option to do so using a cache that is maintained in the C drive on a per-project basis. The cache has a limit of 4 GB for each desktop platform application (though notice that it is actually possible to set a smaller cache value via code). Asset bundles are loaded via the **WWW.LoadFromCacheOrDownload** method from the Unity API, which swiftly retrieves the information if it's already present in the cache, or loads it from the container and stores it in the cache after loading if it's not.

SPM uses asset bundles both for storing the assets used throughout the UI and for the layers used in the mission animations. The UI assets are grouped together into bigger asset bundles (e.g., all the pictures for the various programs are stored under a single bundle named Programs.unity3d), whereas the individual layers used for the mission animations are each stored in their own individual bundle. For example, the animation layer "00-01-00_01Alpha.png" is stored inside an asset bundle named "00-01-00_01Alpha.unity3d".

-The pictures highlighted in red are the programs that belong to the "Two Crew Ballistic Capsules" program category, and are all stored in the same asset bundle.-

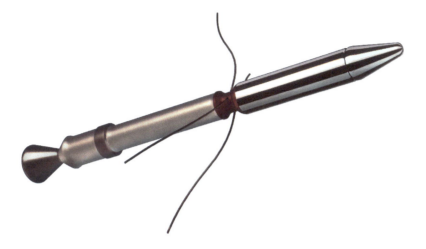

-The "00-01-00_01Alpha" layer used for the mission animations.-

The UI asset bundles are loaded when the game starts, which might take a few seconds. The upside is that this procedure only needs to be performed only once. All subsequent initialisations are instantaneous since the data is already cached.

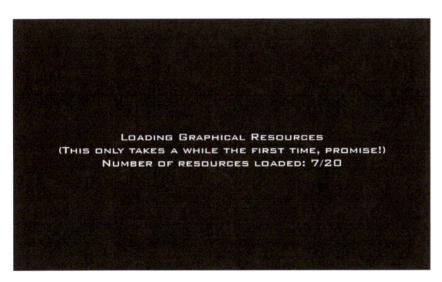

LOADING GRAPHICAL RESOURCES
(THIS ONLY TAKES A WHILE THE FIRST TIME, PROMISE!)
NUMBER OF RESOURCES LOADED: 7/20

-Resources loading screen.-

As mentioned before, the layers used for the mission animations are stored in individual asset bundle files. Originally, I thought about grouping them on a per-mission basis, but then I quickly realised this was going to be terribly inefficient, since many of those layers (e.g., "xxEarth05Flat") are used across multiple missions, and it doesn't make sense to have the same layer stored multiple times across various asset bundles.

-The "xxEarth05Flat" layer is used across multiple animations.-

The asset bundles approach worked quite well for us on the desktop version of the game. However, it had one drawback that made it unsuitable for the mobile port. More specifically- the cache takes a lot of disk space. As mentioned before, its maximum size can be setup via code but, if a very small value is used, it will rarely contain the requested assets, which defeats the purpose of the caching system. Storage in iOS devices is a precious resource, and we were already pushing the envelope quite hard due to the sheer amount of assets contained in the game, so we definitely didn't want to add a couple extra GBs on top of that to account for the local cache. Players would have had to delete several games from their devices to make room for SPM.

Due to the previous reason, it seemed that the asset bundles weren't the way to go for iOS for this particular game. Luckily for us, the iOS platform supports the PVRTC format, which stores compressed textures using only 2 bits per pixel (for comparison, a true colour texture requires 32 bits per pixel). This impressive level of compression enabled us to store everything inside the "Resources" folder instead, thus eliminating the need for a cache and for the lengthy first-time initialisation already present in the desktop platforms. The only caveat is that textures in the iOS version in general, and the mission animations in particular, don't look as crisp as in the desktop platforms due to the high level of compression. This could not be avoided, and it's a consequence of the large number of assets in the game, which in turn is a consequence of the technical decisions I made based on the tools and resources available at that time when I started working on it many years ago.

After solving this and many other technical problems, I managed to get the first version of SPM running on my iPad 3, so I went ahead and let the community know about this via a forum post[22], which was well received. The port was far from ready, as there were still a bunch of technical challenges to overcome, but things were moving forward.

At the end of January, I ran away from the British winter and visited my native Argentina. It was my first visit after more than two years (the last one had been in mid-2012), and during my stay, I worked on the game in the mornings and afternoons and visited friends and relatives during the evenings. In addition to the iOS port, I worked on several other features and enhancements that were meant to be included in the rest of the platforms too.

In early February, we released a beta patch on Steam in order to test these new features (SPM v.1.1.29), which included an in-game tutorial, lots of UI improvements, various bug fixes, and a new "Tiger Team" gameplay mechanic. The "Tiger Team" feature was added to introduce some interactivity to the mission animations by allowing the player to hire a team of paid experts in order to increase the chances of success every time a problem arises. The beta patch feature on Steam was incredibly useful, as it enabled us to try all these (potentially breaking) changes and additions with those players willing to test them, but without running the risk of breaking the game and annoying those players who didn't have an interest to see all these features in advance. We released two more beta patches: SPM v. 1.1.55 and SPM v. 1.2.0, on February 20th and February 27th, respectively, and both of them were key to ensuring that the "official" update would be as bug-free as possible.

-The in-game tutorial, which covers the basics of the game up until the launch of the first mission.-

Closed Beta and iOS Release

(February 2015 - Early March 2015)

In early February we started a closed beta to sort out any potential issues in the iOS version, with participants reporting any issues via a private sub-forum in Slitherine's webpage. Not many people signed up for the beta though luckily the few that did were really committed and provided very useful feedback from the participants. The closed beta also helped us refine the in-game tutorial and the various other elements we were working on which were common to all platforms.

-The distance between the input point and the top-left corner of the tooltip box is greater for touch-based devices than the one used for desktop ones.-

All in all, this stage went relatively smoothly, and most of the reported problems had to do with usability issues. For example, players suggested adding a greater offset to the tooltip boxes to take into account the fact that they can easily get occluded by the fingers.

After getting confirmation from the participants that the game was running fine on their devices, we went ahead and submitted the game for approval to Apple. The release was scheduled for March 12th, and it was important to submit the game several days in advance to take into account that the process can take up to ten days. Moreover, if something goes wrong during the submission, it needs to be addressed and resubmitted, which effectively puts the game back at the end of the queue and it jeopardises the chances of making the game available by the intended date.

Except for a minor hiccup where Apple tried to reject the game because it featured Buzz's name and they weren't aware of the fact that we had the rights to use it, we didn't experience any issues during the review and the game was approved in time for the planned release date. We made the game available on the evening of March 11th (Wednesday) and then... a small crisis ensued! We started getting reports from certain players who claimed they couldn't play the game, were experiencing lockups or were having issues completing the in-game tutorial, how could this be happening?

I started asking for more details in the reports and found out a common pattern; the players who were reporting issues owned either iPad Air or iPad Mini devices. I only owned a (now old) iPad 3 device and all the players who tested the game during the closed beta owned regular iPads too (i.e., no Air or Mini devices). I asked one the guys from Slitherine's Marketing team in the Milan office to give the in-game tutorial a go in one of the iPad Airs on Friday and he confirmed the problem reported by the testers. I couldn't consistently reproduce the problem on my iPad 3, so Slitherine went ahead and ordered an iPad Air for me with expedited delivery so that I could have it the next day, reproduce the problem and, hopefully, fix it.

The iPad Air arrived on Saturday morning and, as expected, I managed to reproduce the problem reported by the various players. This actually made me very happy, as I now had a way to test the potential solutions. Still, I didn't know what the problem was, but, at least I could start working on it.

After some digging, I found that the problem could be related to something called "IL2CPP". In a nutshell, IL2CPP is a system developed by Unity that converts C# code into C++, which is then subsequently compiled natively for a target platform. This brings lots of advantages, such as improved performance and the fact that it becomes easier for Unity to support newer platforms. Here's a brief article[23] which provides an excellent source of information to understand the basics behind IL2CPP.

Development work on IL2CPP was announced by Unity in a blog post[24] from late May 2014, and was made available to the general public as part of Unity 4.6.2, which was released on January 29th, 2015. This was just in time to address Apple's requirements stating that all apps submitted after February 1st, 2015 must include 64-bit support (see this post[25]). I was already aware of the 64-bit requirement, and at some point in February, I started distributing versions of the game built against the IL2CPP backend for the beta testers to try out. Still, no serious issues were reported by the participants, so I assumed that everything was fine.

When looking for a solution to our problems with certain iPad devices, I found out that Unity had been releasing patches on a constant basis featuring tons of bug fixes to address problems reported by fellow iOS developers. I went ahead and downloaded the latest one for 4.6 (4.6.3p3, released on March 13th) and gladly found out that the game was now working properly on both my iPad 3 and the iPad Mini I got a few hours before. I tested the game a bit more and everything looked fine, so I sent an updated build to Slitherine on Monday, which they subsequently submitted to Apple along with a note asking for an expedited review. The updated version of SPM became available a couple of days later in the App Store, and we confirmed that all the stability issues were now gone.

So what had happened? I will never know for sure. For some reason, the IL2CPP bugs were not affecting regular iPad devices and since we only tested the game in those kinds of devices during the closed beta, we never found out about the bugs until the game was released. Lesson learned, next time we'll do a more comprehensive testing process and use a wider range of devices.

Pre-Production Work on SPM 2 and Its Cancellation (March - May 2015)

After submitting the first iOS version to Apple for review and a few days before the "IL2CPP crisis" occurred, I went to Epsom to visit Slitherine's HQ to discuss all the various options and decide what to do next. On the one hand, I really liked the fact that I was able to work on my own projects. Moreover, Slitherine, unlike many publishers out there, always gave me a lot of room to make my own decisions without trying to impose any design decisions or constraints. On the other hand, the sales up to that point hadn't been that great and probably not worthwhile if we took into account the sheer number of hours and all the stress experienced throughout the project. The final decision on what to do next wasn't clear-cut by any means.

Still, Slitherine's owners managed to persuade me to start working on a sequel. And they did so by raising a series of valid points:

- SPM was Polar Motion's first project and, despite being an ambitious project, we had managed to get it out of the door and get an overall positive reception.

- The game wasn't a massive commercial success. Nonetheless, it managed to sell a decent number of copies.

- All the lessons learned throughout the development of the game would have taught us a thing or two about game development, so we should expect a less painful experience when working on a sequel.

From my point of view, the biggest problem with SPM in terms of human resources was that, effectively, I had been the programmer, the designer, and the project manager. Maintaining an online presence across three forums (Matrix Games, Slitherine, and Steam) and exchanging messages with those members of the community who contacted me directly took a considerable amount of time, too. This is a lot to ask for from a single individual, and I'd need to get some help if we wanted the sequel to be commercially successful. To accomplish this, Slitherine paired me up with a game designer who would take some of the workload off from me, so starting in mid-March 2015 we began the pre-production phase of SPM 2.

As I mentioned before, the original plan for SPM was to release a massive game spanning all the way since the dawn of the space age until the first manned mission to Mars. During 2012, we realised that delivering the whole game as a single instalment wasn't a viable option due to the sheer amount of content needed, and that's when we decided to split it into three parts. In theory, since the episode that covered the Lunar Landings had been released, we would start working on an episode focused on space stations around Earth orbit by adding content into the existing codebase. In practice, there were a set of constraints that made this approach a bad idea:

- Producing the in-game animations for the various missions was very expensive.

- The core game mechanics were based on a system that broke down the game elements into "Program Categories", "Programs" and "Mission Configurations". This system was fine for the game I had envisioned back in 2007, where players were meant to follow one of the various fixed paths. But it wouldn't provide the amount of flexibility required for interesting gameplay decisions.

- The graphical resources used for the layered animations had considerable disk space requirements. We were quite lucky in that we managed to fit all of them in the iOS version by using compressed textures that fit in the Resources folder. However, the game as it was had considerable space requirements, and adding twice the existing amount for parts 2 and 3 would be too much.

With those constraints in mind, we decided to start working on the pre-production of a sequel. This stage would last for nearly three months, and we were aiming to create the roadmap for a project that had to be developed in a year and a half, with me being the only programmer again. The sequel was going to be a single-player experience delivered as a single instalment, and its focus would depart from depicting historical elements in excruciating detail and move towards offering lots of gameplay options and replay ability, which is what makes games more interesting. The sequel was going to be more of a reboot, really, as it was meant to start again at the dawn of the space age. For some people, the Race to the Moon was the most exciting period of space exploration, so if we were going to create a new instalment in the series we had to include it as well.

During the following two months, I spent my time reading up on all the information on space stations and lunar bases I could get my hands on. I also spent a considerable amount of time exploring various Unity packages from the Asset Store to cut development costs. Even with all these tasks on my plate, I still found time to read numerous non-fiction books that I had in my backlog and work on various improvements for SPM. Every two weeks I would hop on to the 6:30 AM train to Epsom for a 3+ hour ride and meet with Slitherine's Directors and the game designer they had paired me up with to discuss ideas for the next game. The designer had more background playing and analysing games than I did, and many interesting concepts came out from those meetings.

At some point during the pre-production phase, I realised that things weren't going well, as the project we were planning was too ambitious for an 18-month development schedule and such a small development team. I was already a bit stressed due to having spent years working on SPM on a part-time basis, followed by a very intensive Early Access Program in 2014, which ultimately ended in another intensive period of post-release improvements and the development of the mobile version. Would this new game sell well in today's highly-competitive market? Slitherine's Directors said it would, but I wasn't so sure about it. So in early June, I decided to shelve the project and took up an offer from Unity to work as a Software Developer in their Brighton offices. I relocated at the end of that month and began working there in mid-July.

Pre-productions are all about finding out whether a project plan is viable. In my view SPM 2 felt like a big gamble and, as painful as it was to shelve something you have invested time and money on, it seemed like the right thing to do if I wanted to avoid further losses.

●●●

References:

13. http://www.pockettactics.com/news/ios-news/slitherine-corrects-course-buzz-aldrins-space-program-manager/
14. https://www.youtube.com/watch?v=ppTFYoArCTo&feature=youtu.be
15. http://www.slitherine.com/forum/viewtopic.php?f=226&t=53585
16. https://www.youtube.com/watch?v=me-ilUkhKXY
17. https://www.youtube.com/watch?v=9dR9HXj4zGE&feature=youtu.be
18. http://steamcommunity.com/app/308270/discussions/0/613940477765976853
19. http://steamcommunity.com/app/308270/discussions/0/613940477765976853#c613940477829807604
20. http://steamcommunity.com/app/308270/discussions/0/613940477765976853#c613940477831363940
21. http://www.slitherine.com/forum/viewtopic.php?f=226&t=53774
22. http://www.slitherine.com/forum/viewtopic.php?f=226&t=55279
23. http://www.what-could-possibly-go-wrong.com/il2cpp/
24. http://blogs.unity3d.com/2014/05/20/the-future-of-scripting-in-unity/
25. http://blogs.unity3d.com/2014/11/20/apple-ios-64-bit-support-in-unity/

Part IV

Lessons Learned While Developing SPM

After reading so many post-mortems and articles written by other developers over the last few years, I had long come to the conclusion that there's no silver bullet or universal truth when it comes to game development. Success stories from fellow developers, especially those who have just achieved their first hit, are always interesting and encouraging reads, but I believe there's no conclusive methodology. It is important to keep in mind that whichever approach worked for a given developer might not be applicable to everybody else's situation. Or even anybody else for that matter.

The material presented in the following sub-sections is a compilation of the things I wish I had known when I first started working on SPM, along with some observations I've made during the process. Hopefully, you'll find some useful takeaways in this set of notes.

About the Inception and Pre-Production Phases

The inception and pre-production phases are key to shaping up the overall concept of the project, and many of the decisions made during these two stages can make all the difference between a smooth production and a constant uphill struggle. Some things to keep in mind during the early stages are:

1. **Design with a specific audience in mind, and ask yourself whether that audience is going to be big enough to ensure that the game is going to be a commercial success.** SPM was originally conceived as a relatively simple game with a focus on historical elements, but the audience for such a product didn't turn out to be big enough and we had to shoehorn new gameplay elements to attract a bigger audience. The result is a game with a strong historical flavour

and a moderately deep management system, though not nearly as deep and engaging as if we had designed for more strategic depth from the very beginning.

2. **Do more design up-front, don't rush into coding.** When we started working with Boris in early 2013 on what would eventually become the UI of the released version of the game, we only spent a handful of weeks designing it and left many gaps "for later". What we should have done instead is spend all the time necessary in order to fix that stuff first instead of hoping I'd be able to figure out a solution while writing the code for it. Things are easier to fix on paper than in code.

3. **Plan your game budget based on your requirements, not the other way around.** One of the problems with SPM is that instead of designing a game and coming up with a proper budget to produce it, I ended up building a product based on the people I managed to persuade to join me. Had I done proper planning in the initial stages, I would have either done something in order to get the funds necessary to produce the game following a sensible work schedule or would have concluded that the project wasn't worth pursuing and moved on to something less ambitious instead.

4. **Think about the long term consequences of your technical decisions.** Certain poorly thought technical decisions can have a big impact in the long run. For example, when I decided that we were going to display missions as a series of animated layers instead of using static images, I didn't do a proper assessment of the increased amount of time it would take to produce them in such a content heavy game. This bad decision ended up making the lives of all members of the team unnecessarily harder on a feature that ultimately didn't have a significant impact on the final product, as I reckon that most players at some point eventually start skipping the mission animations.

5. **Spend a lot of time thinking about the various currencies that make the internal economy of the game and their interaction.** In SPM, we initially had the "prestige" and "funds". But then we started introducing more gameplay elements that had an impact on them based on the feedback we got from the Early Access Program and the overall system became a lot less tight because of this. Had I put much more thought into the internal economy of the game early on, I would have been able to catch inconsistencies and fix them before the production phase started, thus avoiding lots of rework.

6. **Don't wait too long until showing your concept and initial ideas to other people.** Unfortunately, for SPM, I literally waited years before discussing the concept behind the game with other people outside my inner circle

of friends and family, none of which is composed by hard-core gamers. I should have done a sanity check with other people outside this circle a lot sooner. Had I done this, I would have probably found out earlier that the product was ill-conceived and that it should have been designed in such a way that has more appeal to strategy gamers.

7. **This piece of advice is probably a corollary of the previous one- if you're planning to partner with a publisher, don't wait too long to start searching for one either.** One of the many good things about having your game distributed by a publishing company is that they have a good understanding of the market and the player base. Thus, by contacting a publisher earlier, you can get the Marketing team involved earlier on and plan your game accordingly. This doesn't mean that you're "selling out" or "doing it for the money". Your games have to sell well if you want to continue making them, and getting marketing involved early on and following some of their advice might make all the difference between a flop and a successfully commercial product.

8. **Design your game so that the first hour of gameplay is extremely engaging and progressively introduces the player to the various elements of the game.** This was a major mistake I made with SPM. During the first stages, the player has to do a lot of busy work such as starting the construction of the various buildings, opening the first program and advancing turns until it's relatively safe to launch the first space mission. Moreover, it might take a solid 20 minutes since the game starts until the first mission is launched, which is far from optimal. Had SPM been a free-to-play game, I seriously doubt most players would play it for more than a handful of minutes before dismissing it.

9. **Design the UI so that it can easily adapt to various screen resolutions and aspect ratios.** Screens for desktop computers and tablets come in a wide variety of shapes and sizes and, to cut development time, it's smarter to design the UI its elements are placed and resized across anchor points instead of designing them with a fixed size. Luckily for us, many of the screens in SPM were just overlays that could be shown on any screen resolution without any modifications, but some for some other screens we actually had to create different versions depending on the aspect ratio, which made the development process error-prone and inefficient.

10. **Make the UI as little asset-intensive as possible.** When designing what would ultimately become the final UI for the game with Boris in early 2013, I completely overlooked the fact that it wouldn't scale well in terms of required assets. For example, in the "Programs" screen inside the Head-

quarters, the game displays a list of mission configurations associated with the currently selected program. This looks very pretty, but it doesn't scale well for programs that have a great number of mission configurations, as the game has to display a great number of unique images, which might bring down the performance on low-end mobile devices. Moreover, from a production point of view, we need to create a unique image for each mission configuration, which is time-consuming and makes the disk space requirements go up unnecessarily.

-Project Gemini has fifteen mission configurations, which are shown in the right hand-side panel.-

11. If things don't seem to move forward during the initial stages or you don't feel the final product is going to be good enough, go back to the drawing board and sort any outstanding issues first. If you still cannot find a solution, shelve the project and move on to something else. Minimise your losses. This one is hard because we think that if we put a bit more effort on our initial ideas instead of lettings them go, everything will eventually pan out. Luckily, I believe I've learned this lesson, and that's why I decided to shelve the development of SPM 2. Obviously we'll never know for sure if that project would have turned out as another failure or not, but to me, everything led me to believe it would. And if Sid Meier cannot get his concept for a dinosaur game right despite investing years on it[27], I shouldn't feel bad about shelving my game concept either.

About the Production Phase

The production phase starts once the concept of the game and all the most important design details have been nailed down. Ideally, before moving to this phase most of the technical unknowns have been de-risked via small prototypes that prove that the biggest technical challenges can actually be overcame. Some "gotchas" to watch out for during this phase include:

1. **Spend a lot of time making the internal tools as streamlined and reliable as possible.** The quality of the tools we use on a daily basis has a great impact on our productivity and even on our mood. If the tools we use to do our work are unresponsive, poorly designed, crash frequently, output cryptic error messages in response to an invalid piece of input, etc., our overall performance decreases, and that has a direct impact on the final quality of our work. When working on a small team with an even smaller budget and a tight deadline it might be tempting to give less priority to the development of the internal development tools because they are not part of the "final game" itself. But bear in mind that developers will spend dozens of hours working with these tools, so getting them right will provide a great amount of benefit in the long run. Focus on the elements that will provide the most leverage, even if they are not part of the final product itself.

2. **Make sure that there's at least one person responsible for maintaining a clear overall vision of the project.** This person needs to keep a critical eye on how things are being done to find ways to streamline the development process and make it more efficient. Constantly monitor the development process and ask yourself whether certain things can be done in a different way in to save time.

3. **Don't rely solely on the feedback you get from the Early Access or early beta testers when it comes to usability.** This was another mistake I made with SPM. I incorrectly assumed that the Early Access Program was going to take care of identifying all the problems with the game and that I would be able to fix them before the final release, yet the "tooltips incident" from the Steam forums proved me wrong. The lesson I've learned is that, irrespective of whether we conduct an Early Access Program in the future or not, I need to have the game exposed to players who have never seen it before and ask for their feedback.

4. **If you decide to go for an Early Access Program, make sure that before you get the program started, you have enough infrastructure in place so that you can provide frequent updates.** You want your early access program to be the stage where you are constantly adding cool features and content on top of a solid foundation. You don't want to be building the foundation while running the early access or, even worse, replacing it.

5. **Try to fix bugs as soon as they are reported.** And when you do, see if you can add some sort of mechanism to prevent similar issues from occurring. For example, every time we got a bug report related to faulty data (e.g., ill-defined data scripts), I added a new extension to the relevant validation tool so that we can a) catch existing instances of the same problem and b) prevent new instances from being introduced in the future.

About the game itself

Space Program Manager is a fully playable game enjoyed by players across the globe and, at the time of this writing, it boasts a healthy 79% of positive reviews on Steam. That being said, the game has its flaws. If I would get the chance of going back in time, these are the things I'd focus on fixing first:

1. **Shift the focus away from the content and the historical factor and spend more time on gameplay.** I've mentioned this lesson in one way or another a few times before, but it's worth going over it again; focusing too much on the historical details and obsessing over minor details from the mission animations was a mistake. This ultimately ended up taking time away that could have been better spent on improving the game balance, polishing the UI or tweaking gameplay elements. Don't get me wrong, I'm quite proud of the level of detail contained within SPM and the fact that it helped many space enthusiasts learn a lot more about the American and Soviet space programs. But, in the end, I think the game could have done a lot better from a commercial point of view had we had focused more on gameplay and less on the historical details.

2. **Let players tell their own story by playing the game.** Another shortcoming of SPM is that the various employees from the space agency don't get enough recognition for what they do. It's also hard for the player to remember which ones participated in the most important events, such as the first astronaut

that performed an orbital flight, or the first one who achieved a successful docking with an uncrewed vehicle. Unlike games like X-Com, where you develop such a strong bond with your soldiers to the point that losing one of them in combat feels really painful, in SPM the player rarely develops such a strong connection with the various employees. If I were to work on the game again, I'd make sure that the player has a unique story to tell on each play through, and that when he completes the campaign he can look back and remember all the special events that occurred.

3. **Make use of existing historical footage.** I always enjoy seeing a picture from a historical event recreated for a different type of media, such as a movie, a mini-series or a computer game. SPM features plenty of images that are based on existing photographs, such as Buzz coming down the ladder of the Lunar Module during the Apollo 11 mission. Personally, I believe there's a certain beauty to them, because when you see them they look very familiar, yet they have a visual style which is unique to the product they belong to. However, based on the feedback we got from the forums, I believe we shouldn't have spent as many resources as we did on recreating existing pictures and, instead, we should have adopted a hybrid approach. This would have taken historical footage along with our own renders to fill in the gaps where no material is available. This was what the original BARIS did, and probably what many fans of the original game expected from SPM too.

-Project Gemini has fifteen mission configurations, which are shown in the right hand-side panel.-

-SPM´s recreation of Buzz Aldrin coming down the ladder of the Lunar Module.-

4. **Let the player adjust the strategy as the game unfolds.** In SPM, once the player chooses a certain strategy (e.g., Project Mercury followed by Gemini and ending with Apollo), they pretty much need to stick to it until the end, even if they experience setbacks along the way. A player can always choose whether to invest more resources in improving the reliability of the various mission components, send its personnel to advanced training to improve their skills or decide to launch a mission sooner in order to beat its opponent and gain more prestige by achieving a given milestone first. But, in the end, it's very hard for the player to change the overall strategy halfway through. While historically accurate, this is not what players expect from a strategy game.

5. **Figure out a way to make the mission execution sequences more engaging from a gameplay point of view.** The mission execution sequences provide a visual "reward" along with some nail-biting moments where the player anxiously hopes that the current mission step succeeds so that he can move closer to the finish line. We then introduced a bit of decision making in a post-release patch by providing the player with the option of hiring a group of paid experts or "Tiger Teams" to increase the chances of success of a given mission step. This provides an element of choice but, ultimately, it's not extremely exciting and leaves the player feeling a bit helpless when things go wrong.

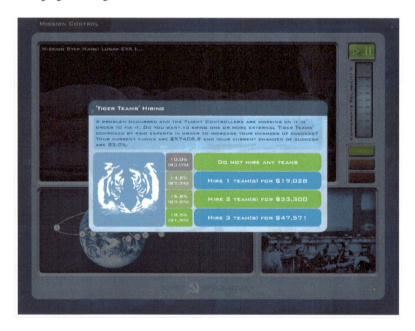

-Players are allowed to hire "Tiger Teams" when something goes wrong in order to minimise the chances of failure.-

6. **The UI.** The UI in SPM can be a bit convoluted at some points. Certain workflows require too many clicks, some functionality is spread across several screens and overlays and there are instances where the game fails to clearly communicate the consequences of the decisions made by the player. This doesn't stop players from enjoying the game, but I reckon that the learning curve is higher than it should be. If I could start working on the game again, I'd certainly pay a lot more attention to this.

7. **The world doesn't feel alive.** In the race to the Moon campaigns, the player gets notifications on what the other faction is up to via the news screen at the beginning of every season, but ultimately it feels like a race where there is no interaction between its competitors. The theme in SPM is a bit unique for a computer game, in the sense that you don't actually "fight" with your competitor. We could always add a "sabotage" mechanic in order to decrease the chances of success of the opposing faction, but it just doesn't feel right for this type of game. Instead, if we were to start the development of the game again, we would make sure that there's more interaction between factions by allowing technology trade or espionage.

-The "News Screen", which is shown at the beginning of every season.-

8. **Not enough stats are provided to the player.** SPM provides some information via its "Museum" building, but ultimately this was a missed opportunity. Players love to see stats, and I think we could have shown a lot more had I taken the time to do more up front design and thinking about the user interface earlier on.

What's Next for Us?

A few months ago Mauricio and I started working on a new space exploration strategy game. Around mid-August, we were joined by Sebastian, a game designer from the SPM community. This new game is solely based on space stations, and its working title is "Space Station Manager" or SSM. In SSM, players control a private space company and compete against other companies to be the first to build and manage an infrastructure in Earth orbit. Yes, we're excited about the premise of Space Station Manager too!

We are consciously applying all the lessons we have learned with SPM and are much more confident we'll get things right this time and minimise the amount of rework during the development phase. Among the pitfalls we're watching out for, we're making sure that the player is constantly confronted with meaningful decisions to make. That the interaction among the various currencies is tight and that the UI is easy to navigate and provides all the information that the players need

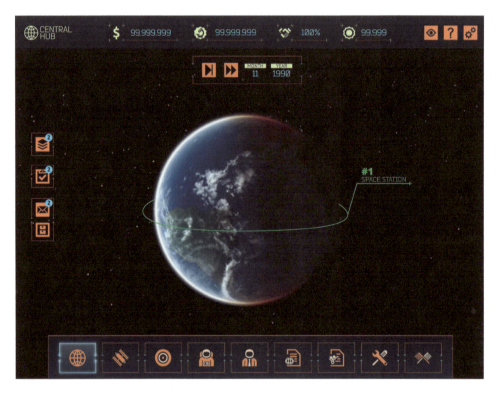

-The Central Hub screen in "Space Station Manager".-

in order to understand the current situation and the outcome of their choices. And even if this new game doesn't do well from a financial point of view, the fact that I now have a steady source of income from my day job at Unity certainly relieves me from all the stress associated with having to depend on the outcome of a single project.

At the time of this writing (mid-December 2015), we're still in the pre-production phase and we expect we will remain in this stage for no less than five or six months. Since there's still a lot of elements we still have to nail down and we don't want to rush into production only to find out, later on, that we need to go back to the drawing board to spend lots of time doing rework due to a major flaw we have overlooked. Reworking major systems during the production phase takes a lot of time which, due to our other commitments, is now a scarce resource, so we are trying to be as efficient as possible.

Sebastian and I are working on the game design and having two meetings on Skype per week in order to discuss the details. We are paying special attention to the mistakes I made during the development of SPM and doing our best to avoid them. For every gameplay mechanic we introduce, we think deeply about how

-The 3D model of the Space Shuttle for "Space Station Manager".-

is that going to affect the UI, how we are going to clearly communicate it to the players, whether it adds an interesting gameplay decision or it's just a meaningless chore for the player to execute, etc. And I always make sure that I bring up the "Things are easier to fix on paper than in code" motto at least once every meeting...

Since the pre-production phase of "Space Station Manager" will take many months, at the end of November 2015, I decided to start working with Mauricio on a smaller version of "Space Station Manager" called "Space Station Designer" or SSD. "Space Station Designer" is a very focused game that will allow players to design their own orbital outposts in Earth orbit while taking into consideration basic requirements such as electricity, heat dissipation, and life support system requirements. A few days after I started writing down ideas for SSD I realised that it might be a good candidate for Virtual Reality devices, so Mauricio and I have shifted the focus and are currently trying to learn as much as we can about this platform and doing experiments on a <u>Gear VR</u>[26] device I've managed to borrow. We're both really excited about working on this smaller project, as it's exactly what we need to keep us engaged while working on the pre-production phase of the much more ambitious "Space Station Manager". Moreover, all the lessons learned on the smaller "Space Station Designer" will be directly applicable to "Space Station Manager".

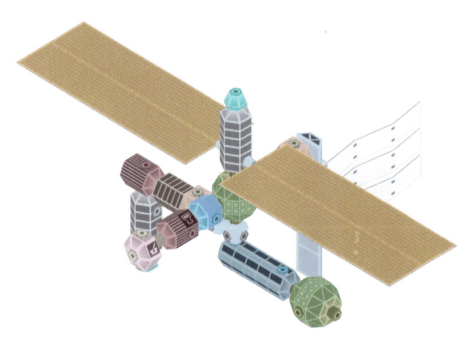

-Concept art for "Space Station Designer".-

We're planning to start a development blog in order to share our experiences developing both games, so stay tuned and follow us on Twitter[28] if you want to know more. In addition to "Space Station Manager" and "Space Station Designer", we continue providing support for "Space Program Manager" by releasing updates featuring minor fixes and enhancements. We have released several updates during 2015 and we're planning to continue doing that during 2016 too.

• • •

References:

26. https://www.oculus.com/en-us/gear-vr/
27. http://flashofsteel.com/index.php/2005/05/20/games-that-never-were-sid-meiers-dinosaurs/
28. https://twitter.com/PolarMotion

EPILOGUE

Final Thoughts and Closing Comments

Space Program Manager was certainly a big project. By revisiting all the various twists and turns that transpired during the last eight years, I realise that, in the end, we were quite lucky that the game eventually saw the light of day. Unfortunately, the number of sales didn't live up to our expectations but, in any case, by working on SPM I gained a lot of experience in various areas, met Buzz Aldrin in person and I can proudly claim that I have programmed an entire multi-platform strategy game on my own. SPM might not have panned out as we expected from a commercial point of view, but it certainly taught us a few lessons that we'll apply in the development of "Space Station Designer" and "Space Station Manager", and I'm confident we'll get both games right this time.

ABOUT THE AUTHOR

Ignacio Liverotti is a Software Developer based in the city of Brighton and Hove in the United Kingdom. Born and raised in Argentina, he emigrated to the UK a couple of years after earning his Computer Science Engineering degree from the Buenos Aires Institute of Technology (ITBA). He held a variety of software development roles in various companies and is currently employed at Unity Technologies.

www.ingramcontent.com/pod-product-compliance
Lightning Source LLC
Chambersburg PA
CBHW041427050326
40689CB00003B/688